Sacred Renewal

Embracing the Biblical Design for Self-Care

S.T. Arriaga

Sacred Renewal: Embracing the Biblical Design for Self-Care

© 2025, S.T. Arriaga

To request permissions, contact the publisher at
ithirialrisingpress@gmail.com

ISBN: 978-1-962896-02-7

First Paperback Edition: July 2025

Cover art and internal design
Kadesh Ink Author Services
Cover image by girleaiulian courtesy of Deposit Photos
Spirit Fire Life Logo by Hineni Asah Creations
Author portrait by Picture This! Photography, used with permission.

Scripture quotations are based on the World English Bible (WEB), which is in the public domain. Certain names have been rendered using the sacred names for consistency with the author's usage. No other textual changes have been made.

Printed in the U.S.A.

Dedicated to my Elohim, my Father, my King.

Who and what would I be without You?

*Thank You for never giving up on me,
thank You for allowing me to hear Your voice.
Thank You for freeing me.*

*Thank You for giving me a voice,
thank You for turning my sorrowful rags
into beautiful flowing robes
of joy, peace, and love.*

*I am not worthy, but I will be forever thankful for
Your hand in my life and Your Spirit whispering in my heart.
I pray that the works of my hands are a sweet fragrance before You, and
that you will always delight and rejoice over me.*

Table of Contents

INTRODUCTION

"If I am not for myself, who will be for me?
If I am only for myself, what am I?
If not now, when?"

Avot 1:12

Self-care and self-love have been topics that I have struggled with for many years. Both are concepts that are difficult for me to grasp because of childhood trauma and the dysfunctional adaptations that I developed in order to survive and function in the world.

While it always seems easy for me to pinpoint and give advice to others in these two areas, having these foundations in my own personal life was never even a thought. That was until I had a nervous breakdown in 2014 that set me on an entirely new path of self-discovery and healing.

After several years of therapy, I was finally strong enough to leave the environment that had made me sick in the first place, and then I spent the next several years learning how to live in freedom. The challenges of living far from everything I had ever known, and learning an entirely new culture consumed many more years during which I fell back into old patterns of thinking, co-dependence, and allowing myself to be consumed with another high-powered, high-stress career that I love, but was slowly killing me from the inside out.

I became more depressed, anxious, and exhausted as every second passed, and I remember feeling like no one cared that what they needed or required of me was too much. I resented the assumption that those in my life had as they made plans for me, took my time and efforts for granted, and never allowed me to say no.

I knew something needed to change, but I couldn't quite put my finger on it. While I had a feeling that I was part of the problem, I didn't know what could be done to change the cycles I had always found myself in. I was too close to the situation and was blind.

The Summer of 2022 brought more change and beautiful blessings to my life. The COVID pandemic was winding down and our lives were returning to normal, and YHVH sent me the man that would become my husband. Through his unconditional love and acceptance of me, the way he cared for me without coddling or pandering, and his encouragement, I learned to see myself as so much more than a commodity to be used, and my journey of self-love, self-care, and acceptance began.

Giving myself permission to care for myself before others is still a struggle for me, and there are still times when I need reassurance that I am not sinning by taking care of my needs before taking care of everyone else. As I have grown in this area, I have begun to understand the roots of these negative beliefs that were initially instilled in me by well-meaning, God-fearing believers when I was a child. Slowly and surely, I have begun pulling the weeds and learning how to cultivate a balanced, Scriptural view of what it means to be a good steward of my body, mind, and spirit.

Learning and applying self-love and self-care have permeated our popular culture in recent years. The discussion birthing countless books, articles, discussions, and posts on our social media feeds that show the benefits from both spiritual and mental health standpoints. However, if you've experienced well-meaning teachings or unhealthy environments that teach that anything that puts the "self" first is sinful at worst and selfishness at best, then you understand the negative feelings that I have internalized and acted from in every area of my life.

The truth is, that self-care and self-love are topics that Scripture is very clear on, but because it is often taught from a new age or secular worldview rather than a Biblical one, it sometimes becomes hard to discern what is balanced or correct in YHVH's eyes. Not only can these concepts feel threatening to us personally, but they can also feel threatening to our faith. As a result, many of us reject these ideas completely as non-Biblical, while others try to reconcile and understand without adopting non-Scriptural beliefs. The bottom line is, there are a lot of things we have been misunderstanding for a very long time, and it requires some painful work to make the corrections, which often leaves us feeling defeated and unable to change.

So how do we reconcile the knowledge of mental health and self-prioritization, without making it worse with over-correction, or by continuing to live in denial or ignorance of what YHVH calls us to be? Is it possible to put ourselves appropriately first, and is it Biblical to do so? Are self-love and self-care compatible with a life devoted to YHVH, or are they too great of a risk to attempt to balance because they may lead to selfishness and pride? This book is the exploration of the path that my own questions took me on. Questions that have guided me to a deeper understanding of how self-love, self-respect, and care for my well-being is directly aligned with living a life that glorifies our Creator.

Please join me as I explore the different facets of self-love and self-care. Together we will explore Scriptural insights, practices and reflections that can help us understand and integrate these Biblical principles into our daily lives in a balanced and healthy way. Together, we will examine what it means to see ourselves through YHVH's eyes, embrace humility in the care of ourselves, and appreciate His design for us while ensuring that we care for the mind, body, and spirit He entrusted us with. Through this study, we will discover that true self-love is less about self-importance, and more about honoring YHVH and being healthy and fit to be the vessels of His love in a world that so desperately needs it.

In this book, I have chosen to use the Hebrew Tetragrammaton (יהוה) or YHVH when referring to the Name of the Almighty. This decision is made with respect for the diversity of pronunciation and traditions within the Messianic and Hebrew Roots communities. My intention is not to prescribe a specific pronunciation but to honor the reverence and significance of our Creator's Great Name.

May we draw ever closer to the heart of our Creator, and learn to care for ourselves properly, so we can love others more freely and genuinely.

~ S.T. Arriaga, 2025

DIAGNOSING THE SICKNESS

For You formed my inmost being.
You knit me together in my mother's womb.
I will give thanks to You,
for I am fearfully and wonderfully made.
Your works are wonderful.
My soul knows that very well.

Psalms 139:13-14

From the very beginning of creation, Scripture tells us that we were created in the image of Elohim ([1]Genesis 1:26-27). That we are unique and have worth that deserves respect and care. However, somewhere in our development, many of us begin to take the importance of caring for ourselves out of the equation for a multitude of reasons. It could be due to our family dynamics, unsafe situations that have scarred us, events that have planted bad seeds that grew into poor self-esteem or misunderstood Biblical teachings. The list of the symptoms is much longer than I could include here, but the resulting sickness is the same. We learn to make ourselves small, learn to not make space for ourselves in our relationships and lives. We begin to adopt co-dependent and passive aggressive patterns in our relationships. We find our hearts and minds are constantly stressed, anxious, and overwhelmed. No matter where we turn, we begin to attract or keep the toxic people in our lives that fuel the cycle. We find ourselves in bondage to what people think of us. *We become people pleasers instead of YHVH pleasers.*

Somewhere along the way, we stop recognizing and understanding that we carry the image of Elohim into the world. We can't fathom that self-love and self-care are not acts of pride but are instead acts of *celebration* and *appreciation* for the very breath that Elohim breathed into us. We begin to feel guilty for saying no or not doing our best for others 100% of the time even while knowing we can't. All the while resenting the activities and people that we promise our time and energy to as we slowly but surely deplete our emotional, physical, and mental resources. It is a vicious, seemingly endless cycle that feels harder to escape than to continue.

I was raised in a super conservative, independent Pentecostal family in small town Minnesota. Our family group was deeply enmeshed after generations of secrets and trauma. I feel that while the spiritual walks of my family members are genuine and heart-felt, their faith walk also became a mask for the pain. A way to detach, justify, and rationalize not being able to stop the cycles, *if* they were even able to recognize them. The family's reputation as strong Christians was to be protected at all costs. There were high expectations for me as all of the women of my family were in church ministry. I watched them give everything of themselves to those around them. My mother and grandmother spent countless hours together, writing and teaching curriculums and Bible study programs to every demographic in attendance. They both volunteered extensively in the community. I was very young when, "there is no excuse if you are able to do it", was instilled in me and I have heard that voice in my head every day since. Driving me to push harder, do more, and never say no to meeting the needs of those around me, no matter what cost I paid.

I already had a low sense of self after years of being physically, emotionally, and sexually abused, so it wasn't a giant leap to think that everyone else was more important than I was. My life consisted of making myself valuable by *doing* in order to be loved. That was my main drive in life well into my late 30's when the resentment and anger of continually being powerless in my own life started giving me the strength to say no and stick to it. The shame and guilt of not "giving my all" and being a "bad example" of YHVH's light to the world was overwhelming. It was spirit-crushing, and often still drove me to saying yes to things I knew I couldn't or didn't want to do. I also began losing people in my life, and because I had become so anxiously attached, I didn't equate it to them leaving because I was birthing boundaries and change in my life. Instead, I saw it as more evidence that I was not worthy of love, and that no matter what I would ever do, I would always find myself abandoned and alone. I saw myself as a commodity that was tolerated until it outlived its usefulness. My mantra of "everybody leaves" became even more solidified in my life. I distracted myself by working harder, giving in to the demands of the ones I love, pushing myself further. I ignored my body and mind screaming for help and relief from the never-ending pressure I was putting on myself. I put my head down and pushed forward the best I could with what little inner resources I had left.

To say that I ran from my hometown in Minnesota after 30 years of living there is an understatement. I was running from a community that had known me for the majority of my life. While I had prided myself on the amount of healing I had accomplished while still in the environment that had injured me, somewhere inside I knew that I needed to take *any* chance to escape if I had any hope of finding true freedom. The tricky part of healing and recovery is that the people that have known us for so long often cannot handle or refuse to see us as anything other than what we have been. Usually, it is because they are benefiting from our lack of boundaries. Which makes true change seemingly impossible, more painful and difficult. Though these people love us, they often can't recognize the negative impact they have as they are searching to fill the voids in their own lives.

The greatest struggle of my life has been my faith walk. Mainly because I was surviving terrible things I didn't understand as a child. While I didn't directly blame YHVH, I also had a sense that I was bad somehow and deserved whatever terrible things happened to me. I had a very deep faith, and always a sense of His presence in my life, but like many of us, I didn't see Him as *Abba Father*. I saw Him as a passive player that watched, comforted and encouraged me, but didn't find me quite "good enough" to rescue. I couldn't accept who He says I am in His Word because I didn't see myself as His child or a work of His amazing craftsmanship. I couldn't fathom that I had a unique calling that He had specifically placed on me, or that He had created me for a beautiful purpose. But I also couldn't stop seeking Him, and for that reason alone I am deeply thankful that I had that need to strive for His love. I didn't realize I already had it, but it was that drive that continued to keep me seeking Him and eventually finding the healing and restoration that He had intended for me all along.

Like Jacob, I wrestled with Him, seeking answers, challenging and pushing back. That determination to understand *why* became the very thing that liberated me and eventually led me to leave Christianity and begin to walk in Yeshua's footsteps. It was the part of me that all the abuse had never managed to destroy, and that tenaciousness became my key to freedom.

I would love to say that my escape to Texas was the ending of my fairy-tale, but it wasn't. Instead, the first four years of growth were painful and hard. I had left everything I had ever known to save myself and ended up in a strange land.

While I had prepared myself for the differences in climate, I had never considered the difference in culture, pace of life, and the stranger I was meeting in myself for the first time. I felt stunted, emotionally immature, and incapable of the growth I desired for myself. I sounded like the children of Israel as they wandered in the wilderness, desperate to go back to Egypt because it was a world I understood, and I knew what role to play. I didn't know how to fight for myself, I didn't know how to get rid of my slavery mindset. I violently cried multiple times a day for the first two years. As time passed the tears slowed, and I gained my footing. I returned to the patterns I had run from in a new place, with new people, but in completely similar situations. I found myself a new job that is a great calling, but I allowed it to consume me for nearly four years.

Because I work in the healthcare system, self-care is a constant topic of conversation. As healthcare workers we constantly pour into others, working long hours and sometimes weeks without days off. When the pandemic hit and our facility was shut down, the pressure and stress became even harder to manage as we struggled to meet the needs of our aging population and the emotional toll it was taking on them as they were removed even further from the world.

Rest and sleep became even more important as we navigated the uncertainty of what was happening in the world, and self-care was still discussed, but not to the same extent. There just wasn't time, we were in survival mode. People began to burn out and leave jobs that they had been passionate about for 25+ years as we struggled to minister to the additional needs of our residents while satisfying the needs of families that were struggling with being kept from their loved ones.

By the time restrictions were lifted we were exhausted and overwhelmed. Once again, self-care became the priority, but it was still something I didn't understand *for myself* until the summer of 2022 when I met the man I would marry the following year. Through his actions and his example, he encouraged me to practice self-care, let him take care of his own emotional self-regulation, and see to my own needs because I *deserved to be happy.* He was the first person to show me that not only was there space for me in our relationship, but also that his expectation was that I would make meeting and communicating my needs a priority. Suddenly I had a new role that didn't fit with being a "fixer" a "people manager" or "people pleaser". I had autonomy and importance as an individual and I was still loved, flaws, wounds, scars and all!

It was a dramatic learning curve for me, but slowly I began to see that I had been given a misunderstanding of what self-care is. And deeper still, for the first time I was able to fully comprehend how I abandoned myself daily and had a lack of love for myself because of unhealed wounds. I had spent years of my life covering layers of scars by overcompensating for my internal sense of worthlessness by pouring endlessly into others. By ignoring my own needs, I had unknowingly fueled and reinforced the toxic and dismissive ideas I had about my value and my place in the world. When clarity finally came, it felt much too late, as I had already burned out, lost my job, and many of the gains I had made personally and professionally as I had rebuilt myself and my life in Texas.

It was a dark time for me, but it was the final piece I needed to finally give myself permission to view myself as a human being worthy of love, freedom, and healing.

It seems almost elementary that it took me so long to learn my worth, when we can so easily see that both YHVH and Yeshua clearly stated it in a commandment, *"you shall love your neighbor as yourself"* ([2]Leviticus 18:18, [3]Matthew 22:39). This is a direct statement, but for most of us, it conflicts deeply with what life has taught us. However, all through Scripture we can see that our love for others is *connected* and *influenced* by the love that we hold for ourselves. For me, this suggests that healthy self-love is not only acceptable, but it is necessary if we are to love and minister to others effectively.

In [4]1 John 4:7-8 we are told that YHVH is love, and that He manifested His love for us through sending His beloved Son to earth so that we could be saved. His love is transformative. It is alive! Through His true, unconditional love, we are saved, changed and renewed. As we grow and heal, we show His light, the gift of His restoration, and then it is spread to those around us. Our lives become a testimony of hope and overcoming. But first, we must *accept* His love. We must learn to see ourselves through His eyes. The eyes of a loving Father.

While modern society and the church often equate self-love and care with personal indulgence or allowing our selfish wants and desires to distract us, Scripture presents a much different picture that is not that shallow. Instead, it is rooted in humility, good stewardship, and community. Self-care YHVH's way is not about indulgence, excess, or selfish self-prioritization, but instead it is about being *present* in our lives. It is about being mindful and caring for our own physical, emotional, and spiritual well-being. Yeshua Himself kept this practice in the Gospels when He withdrew from the crowds and His disciples to pray and rest after ministering. Even though He is the Son of YHVH, He still needed those times of solitude, renewal, and rest so He could continue to serve His flock with strength and compassion. If we are to walk as He walked, we can see that it is not a sin to take care of oneself when in service to the Kingdom of YHVH. Our energy is not boundless, and we cannot serve His purpose if we are exhausted, in a hurry, and unable to pour anything else from our self-abandoned mind, body, or emotions.

When we study the Feasts and Festivals, there is so much we

can learn about how self-care fits in with the rhythms and practices of keeping Torah. It starts with Shabbat and can be seen in Yom Kippur and Rosh Hashanah. In fact, in nearly every set apart time, YHVH declared High Sabbaths, sacred times for rest, reflection, renewal, and reconnection with Him and our faith community. These appointed times are full of joy, but they also allow us to step away from the crush of our daily lives to reconnect with Him others. It gives us dedicated time to nurture both our bodies and our souls. When we obey and observe these practices, we find rest and renewal not only for our own sake, but also as a way of honoring and remembering YHVH's commandments. Obedience to the rhythm YHVH has created for us, becomes an island of rest that allows us to return to our daily lives, prepared to serve with willing and rested hearts and minds.

Learning to see self-love and self-care as an essential part of the rhythm of my faith walk makes all the difference in how I perceive providing and allowing myself space to minister to my own needs. It also helps me to avoid two impulses: self-neglect and self-absorption. We all know where self-neglect leads: burnout, resentment, health problems, and more. All these things begin to diminish our ability to not only hear YHVH's voice but distract us from His call upon our lives as we stretch ourselves thinner and thinner in the attempt to be everything to everyone. Likewise, self-absorption easily blinds us with pride and excess, causing us to be distracted from YHVH's heart for others. Our brothers and sisters in Messiah, our children, spouses, and those He is calling us to shine for are affected by both scenarios. It is up to us to have wisdom, discernment, and a healthy perspective of self-care. If we can learn to see self-care and rest as a gift from YHVH, it becomes a *celebration* and acceptance of His design for us. It becomes exactly what He intended it to be and leads us closer to His heart.

Personal Reflections:

1. What lies have you been told by yourself and others that lead you to believe that you are not deserving of self-love and consideration? What life experiences are linked to these beliefs?

2. How are you self-abandoning? What needs do you have that you ignore? What are the excuses you make to justify why you ignore them?

3. If there is one area of your life that you could change, what would it be? How can self-care and self-love impact it?

4. Make a list of all the thoughts that cross your mind when you try to make time for yourself in your busy life. Are there scriptures that you can use to combat them?

5. What is your goal in reading this book – how would radical self-love and self-care impact your daily life, sense of self and satisfaction?

REFRAMING THE FOUNDATION

Elohim said, "Let's make man in our image, after our likeness....
Elohim created man in His own image.
Male and female He created them.

Genesis 1:26-27

The world's version of self-love often leads to the flesh interpreting it as a free pass for self-centeredness. In contrast, YHVH's definition of self-love is an invitation to embrace our value as His *handmade* image-bearers. He intended for us to pursue a deep *relationship* with Him, to be *filled* with His Spirit, which guides us to compassion, humility, and upright living. So how can we frame self-love in a way that is honoring to our Creator, and learn to correctly see how self-care, humility, and service come together?

It is a direct command of *"love your neighbor as yourself"* in [1]Leviticus 19:18, and Yeshua dives even deeper by stating that it is the second greatest commandment ([2]Matthew 22:39). I began to wonder, if we cannot practice self-love and self-compassion, how are we capable of extending compassion, patience, empathy, forgiveness, and grace to others? Especially toward people that have wounded us, or live lifestyles that we don't understand or would not choose for ourselves?

I believe that Yeshua's emphasis on this commandment shows that love, both for ourselves, and others, is central to YHVH's law. And the truth is that without a genuine sense of self-love, we cannot truly fulfill the commandment of loving others. While one can argue that we can love while hating ourselves, the question becomes, are we able to love *unconditionally* from that place? Can we truly love without unhealthy attachment, or genuinely if we are unable to exercise love and compassion for ourselves? If we do not see ourselves worthy of love, are we capable of experiencing and extending it to its fullness?

To truly love, we need to understand that self-love is about having *proper respect* for ourselves as YHVH's creation. With all the talents, quirks, qualities, flaws, weaknesses and more that He has built into us. In everything that He created, man's creation was so important and intricate that He formed us with His own hands and breathed His own Spirit into us ([3]Genesis 2:7). Does that alone not speak of incredible value? Does that alone not indicate that just in our *existence,* we are important to Him? If we can truly grasp this, I believe we embrace our own worth, and it will become natural to care for our own well-being in a way that is not rooted in selfishness.

In Scripture, we can see that self-love can be paired with humility, that one does not cancel the other. This is the opposite of what many of us are taught, either in church, or as we move through life and interact with others. I was raised to believe that self-love and self-esteem were a direct threat to my salvation. That self-esteem was a slippery slope, the evil opposite to humility that would lead to my demise if I bought the lie. But it was a different lie that I was being taught. Instead, Paul is clear in his writing to the Philippians, that humility doesn't detract from our sense of self-worth or need to care for ourselves with wisdom, instead, it is anchored in the character of YHVH.

"If therefore there is any exhortation in Messiah, if any consolation of love, if any fellowship of the Spirit, if any tender mercies and compassion, make my joy full by being like-minded, having the same love, being of one accord, of one mind; doing nothing through rivalry or through conceit, but in humility, each counting others better than himself; **each of you not just looking to his own things, but each of you also to the things of others.***"*
Philippians 2:1-4 [Emphasis mine]

While most teachings tend to focus on *"each counting others better than himself,"* Paul is teaching about having a humble heart, free from ambitions that are self-centered. Instead, the humility that he speaks of is not about ignoring our own needs, but rather it is about seeing ourselves as part of something bigger. A body, that moves as one, a body that ministers to itself, and sees to its needs ([4]1 Corinthians 12).

Imagine what the modern-day church would look like if we practiced care for our people the way we should. Imagine how brightly our light would shine if we moved as one, caring for each other as one being, moving together in our gifts, and being directed by the Spirit of YHVH! That is why the early church moved with power, because they understood that they were important pieces of a whole that had great purpose.

Marriage language is used all through Scripture to describe YHVH's relationship with His people. In this instance, marriage is also the perfect example of what Paul is speaking of here. When you picture a healthy, strong marriage, it is about each spouse serving the needs of the relationship, and giving to one another out of love, respect, and without obligation or resentment. They support each other in their weaknesses and celebrate each other's strengths. Yes, it is unrealistic to expect our spouses to meet all our needs, so some needs are met in our faith community, our friendships, and our family connections. Yes, sometimes needs must be communicated to one another as having a servant's heart and giving love doesn't magically make us mind-readers. But if a marriage partner is seeking to minister to the other in genuine love and consideration, and the other responds in kind, it becomes a cycle that gains momentum and becomes easier to maintain. It becomes two moving as [5]*echad*/one. It becomes love in action.

In Scripture, humility is not thinking of yourself as less than or not worthy of caring for. Even in Paul's letter, he isn't saying to think poorly of oneself in order to raise others in your esteem. When we do this, we risk placing people on pedestals in our lives. Instead, he simply says, *"each counting others better".* A healthier viewpoint would be to learn how to humble ourselves by not basing our worth on our status, successes, failures, or personal achievements. Instead, basing our sense of self-worth accurately and being content in, and attentive to who we are in YHVH's view ([6]Psalms 8:3-5). In Romans 12:3 Paul tells us:

> *"For I say thorough the grace that was given to me, to everyone who is among you, not to think of yourself more highly than you ought to think; but to think reasonably, as יהוה has apportioned to each person a measure of faith."*

As we know, we are all sinners and have fallen short of YHVH's glory ([7]Romans 3:23), but this does not mean that we cannot exercise self-care or do not deserve to have a peaceful life. It is simply a reminder that we are not greater than any other man or woman, instead, we are part of a beautiful tapestry of love and redemption that is being woven by the Creator of us all!

Because we are each knit together by YHVH's own hand, deeply known by Him, and are created in His image, we can see ourselves as ambassadors and lights to the world and created for the purpose He has intended for us. This view, when tempered with wisdom and discernment, can compel us to value ourselves and others with proper dignity and honor. Just as our U.S. Constitution acknowledges that every person carries inherent worth and respect, we too can learn to respect the choices of others even while not agreeing with them. We can learn to exercise kindness and grace even when it isn't "deserved", and we can have that promised *"peace beyond understanding"* ([8]Philippians 4:7) in a life that is often difficult and challenging. If we can see our value, then it becomes an easy leap to steward our lives well, not for our glory, but for YHVH's. Not for our purposes, but in thankfulness and gratitude for what He has given us.

I propose that if we can truly understand that our individual worth is first directly linked to our *identity* as His creation, and second, to our *relationship* with Him, then self-love becomes an *extension* of His love for us. It becomes a way that we show appreciation and care for His handiwork. By caring for all that He has given us, starting from homebase - our body, soul, mind ([9]Deuteronomy 6:4-5) - we accept His unconditional love. A never-ending unconditional love that He extends to us daily through His covenants, and ultimately, through the sacrificial gift of His only begotten son!

Through this lens, we can freely seek personal growth, nurture our talents, care for our bodies and recognize YHVH's continuous presence in our lives without it becoming unbalanced or sinful. The journey of personal growth, healing, and integrity are part of YHVH's purpose for us as we learn to free ourselves from the *"old man"* and become His *"new creation"* ([10]Ephesians 4:22-24, [11]2 Corinthians 5:17), and it is also how we exercise self-respect and spiritual maturity, which is rooted in self-love!

YHVH clearly outlines His expectations for His people in the

Torah regarding our physical health, rest, clean living, and spiritual renewal. While our modern Western thinking has taught us to regard His laws as unnecessary, in this author's humble opinion, one of the reasons it is difficult for some is because it is not kept in love for our Creator, or in appreciation for all He has done for us! It quickly becomes burdensome when we remove our understanding of His vastly deep love for us! When we view Torah as a love letter from a Father who wants to keep His children safe and healthy, we can see that self-care is essential to our spiritual walk.

Personal Reflections:

1. How does the command to *"love your neighbor as yourself"* from Matthew 22:39 shape your view of self-love? What does this commandment teach about the relationship between caring for yourself and caring for others?
2. In what ways does recognizing that you are made in the image of Elohim (Genesis 1:26-27) impact your sense of self-worth and purpose?
3. How does humility play a role in self-love and self-care? Are there areas in your life where you struggle to balance humility with healthy self-respect?
4. What does it mean to you personally to love yourself? What thoughts contradict this idea?

BALANCING THE LOVE
FOR SELF AND OTHERS

"Even as the Father has loved Me, I also have loved you.
Remain in My love."

John 15:9

Yeshua's teachings on love and compassion are taught by many world religions for a reason. While they see Him as only a prophet and example of empathetic and sacrificial living, as followers of The Way, we have a deeper understanding of who He is and why He taught as He did.

His teachings on love and compassion, while often only equated to the love of others, also offer a better understanding of the relationship between self-care and self-love, while still being in service to others. Unlike modern self-care approaches that may be more focused on meeting our selfish needs, Yeshua's example shows us love as an *overflow* of YHVH's presence in our lives. Walking in His presence will guide us to balance care of ourselves with the care and compassion for others. Yeshua demonstrated a life that was deeply rooted in who YHVH is, and who He is in His identity as His son. He showed by example that it is possible to be set apart and fully redeemed, even while in a flawed body. He calls us to walk as He did, in humility, kindness and service. And yet, even in service

He didn't neglect keeping the Sabbath, and also had times where he intentionally chose rest and prayer, giving us an example of how self-care can exist alongside selflessness.

In Matthew 22:38-39, Yeshua was asked what commandment was the greatest. He responded by quoting [1]Deuteronomy 6:5,

> *"Yeshua said to him, "'You shall love* יהוה *your Elohim with all your heart, with all your soul, and with all your mind.' This is the first and great commandment. A second likewise is this, 'You shall love your neighbor as yourself.' The whole law and the prophets depend on these two commandments."*

Here He highlights that loving ourselves is secondary to loving YHVH, but also that love of self is essential for fulfilling our calling to love others well ([2]Leviticus 19:18).

I think this is a beautiful example of how well YHVH understands us as His creation. As we grow and develop, we begin to have a sense of self and a sense of how we fit in the world. We are all very young when we begin to be taught The Golden Rule, "treat others how you would like to be treated," which is rooted in Deuteronomy 6:5. We each have our own way of experiencing or recognizing love from others in our unique love languages. We all know how we desire or expect to be treated, so it is a beautiful way for us to relate to this lesson.

When we consider Yeshua's words, the phrase, *"as yourself"* it is easy to understand based on us each knowing how we want to be loved and how we want to receive love. We each have experiences in which we have been treated poorly, have experienced embarrassment and shame. We know how we *don't* like to be treated. This is the foundation of empathy.

So how does this apply to self-love and self-care, you ask? Through this idea, we can conclude that loving others *does not exclude* taking care of ourselves, just as Yeshua doesn't imply that we should prioritize ourselves over others. Rather, it presents self-love as the foundation or example of how we are to express outward love. How we esteem ourselves and how we would like to be treated is an excellent gauge for how we should treat others.

Without a healthy, YHVH-centered sense of self, we can find ourselves on dangerous ground without proper boundaries, which will produce burnout, resentment and inadequate care for ourselves and those around us. It also can be a dangerous breeding ground in which we learn to abuse others based off our past traumas, fears, or lack of empathy.

So where do we find this healthy balance? Yeshua's example shows us how He handled caring for others and caring for Himself. While He ministered to the countless, pressing needs of others: healing the sick, feeding the hungry, raising the dead, and teaching spiritually starving crowds, He also made time to withdraw and care for His own needs. And He never apologized for it. He chose to care for Himself. Once refreshed and strengthened by solitude and prayer, He continued on His mission to set the captives free.

In [3]Mark 1:35, after teaching and ministering to the sick, He rose early in the morning to pray alone. Also, in [4]Matthew 14:23, after feeding the 5,000 spiritually and physically, He sends the disciples away and retreats to the mountainside by Himself.

His actions show that self-care is not a luxury, but a necessity. By taking time alone, He not only replenished His physical strength, but reconnected with His Father through prayer. His example shows us that *intentional* periods of rest and connection with YHVH are vital to sustaining a life of service. For us, following in His footsteps means having wisdom and recognizing when we need solitude, prayer, and rest. It is our permission slip to recognize self-care practices as important and beneficial.

Yeshua also called us to be self-sacrificing, and He asked us to take up our cross and follow Him ([5]Matthew 16:24-25). In John 15:13 He says, *"Greater love has no one than this, that someone lay down his life for his friends."* This acknowledgment of sacrificial love is not just about the sacrifice that He had come to make for us. And while it might seem at odds with self-care, it is a powerful example that shows that genuine self-love is not about self-preservation alone, but also involves a willingness to serve others, even at the cost of ourselves.

In Luke 10:25-37. A lawyer asked Yeshua, *"who is my neighbor?"*, and Yeshua's reply is the [6]Parable of the Good Samaritan. There are many lessons we can learn from a deep dive of this parable, but let's focus on a few different details in light of our subject.

The racial identity of the man who fell among robbers isn't given, although it is safe to assume that he was a Jew. In the narrative he is just a person like the 100's of people we randomly cross paths with on any given day. Two described individuals, a priest and a Levite, see him in need, and they not only pass by him, but they also cross over to the other side in order to avoid him. But a Samaritan, who at that time was viewed by Yeshua's audience as filthy and scornful, was the one that loved the stranger and saw to his needs. Even in this parable, the Samaritan does not stop whatever task he was doing, he simply showed mercy and made room in his day for the care of the wounded man. He then continued on his way after ensuring the man would continue to be taken care of. And he checked on him when he returned from completing his journey.

So according to Yeshua's example, true self-love doesn't prioritize personal comforts or desires over YHVH's mission. Being busy doesn't excuse us from doing good. Instead, it offers us the opportunity to not only minister to others, but to do it with wisdom. By helping others from a healthy viewpoint, we are prepared to give generously and compassionately from hearts that aren't overwhelmed or full of obligation. When we see our self-worth through YHVH's eyes, through the eyes of our loving Creator who shaped us from clay and gave us life, we are able to love and serve others without depleting ourselves or losing sight of our own value or other tasks in our daily lives.

Yeshua is not only our Messiah, He is also the embodiment of love, humility, and obedience to YHVH. Through His example, we see that self-care and giving of ourselves can co-exist in harmony. He demonstrated proper balance, where self-love enables the giving of oneself, and when we walk as He did, we ourselves also become examples of the depth of love YHVH has shown us. We become that light to a dying world.

Yeshua's observance of the Sabbath, participating in the Feasts and Festivals, and practice of prayer and time with YHVH, all show the practices that are in line with YHVH's will and purpose for our daily lives. His life was grounded solely in obedience to YHVH's laws and focused on being equipped to serve others. By following in His footsteps, we can see self-care as a tool that helps us fulfill our calling and aligns us with our Messiah's mission of love, reconciliation, and sacrificial love.

All through his letters to the assemblies, Paul continues to encourage believers to practice honest love toward one another. Yeshua also tells us that the world will know us by our love in [7]John 13:34-35. The early believers saw the whole picture of Torah and Yeshua's fulfillment of it, and they understood that it wasn't selfishness to care for their own first.

Torah sets out very specifically how we are to care for each other. It is this internal self-care of the camp that created the light that shone to the nations ([8]Matthew 5:14), and made the world see that the Hebrews were different. Furthermore, through caring for their own, they were able to care for others when the curious or needy sought them out. In this context, self-care becomes part of a larger purpose.

I propose that the highest expression of Biblical self-love always sees its full expression in its ability to *open* us to others. When we view it from this standpoint, it is easy to see that self-love and compassion are not selfish endeavors but instead lead us to being able to love each other well from a stable, healed place. When we find peace, healing, and love for ourselves, we become free to give from the heart, express love in action, compassion and care for others without expectations or rooted in soothing our own internal wounds. This is where we truly learn to walk in sacrificial love as Yeshua did.

Personal Reflection:

1. Yeshua teaches us that we should *"love your neighbor as yourself."* How does this challenge or affirm your current approach to self-love and caring for others?

2. Yeshua showed balance between serving others and taking time for personal restoration. How does His example inspire or encourage you to set boundaries or prioritize self-care in your life?

3. In what ways can you practice self-sacrifice while still maintaining a healthy sense of self-worth and self-compassion?

4. How do Yeshua's teachings on humility and service (Philippians 2:3-4) influence the way you think about self-love and the purpose of self-care?

5. If you are a parent, in ministry, or any other vocation that requires you to care for others, how can you make room in your life to reset and rest? Who in your faith community can you ask for help? Are you able to partner with others in your community to help support each other?

LOVING OTHERS AND
GLORIFYING YAHWEH

"Give, and it will be given to you: good measure, pressed down, shaken together, and running over will be given to you. For with the same measure you measure it will be measured back to you."

Luke 6:38

One of the fundamental principles of Biblical self-care is that it creates an abundance of love, strength, and patience, which allows us to serve others genuinely. In 2 Corinthians 1:3-4, Paul writes:

> *"Blessed be the Elohim and Father of our Master Yeshua the Messiah, the Father of mercies and the Elohim of all comfort, who comforts us in our affliction, that we may be able to comfort those who are in any affliction, through the comfort with which we ourselves are comforted by Elohim."*

Just as a well cannot give water unless it has a spring, we cannot fully love or minister to others if we are spiritually, emotionally, and physically depleted. Practicing self-care through prayer, rest, physical nourishment, enjoyment of hobbies, etc., ensures that we have the resilience to care for others from fullness rather than exhaustion. By embracing self-care and Elohim's rhythm for our lives, we allow Him to fill and renew us with Living Water that will overflow and touch those around us. Self-care is truly the foundation for loving others and having an effective ministry.

One of the challenges of self-love is dealing with our fleshly desires. Our flesh is selfish, self-serving, and seeks its own pleasures at the expense of everything if we allow it. It cries out constantly for its desires to be filled, but as new creatures in Messiah, it is our responsibility to learn how to temper ourselves with self-control. [1]Romans 12:3 advises us to not think higher of ourselves than we should, instead we are told to examine ourselves with sober and sound judgement. True self-love allows us to balance our healthy sense of self-worth with humility because it is grounded in our recognition of our worth as YHVH's creation. In this place we can hold esteem and space for ourselves, while recognizing that we do have needs in our earthly bodies, all while avoiding pride and self-centeredness.

It is humility that teaches us to see ourselves through YHVH's perspective, as loved and valued, but also as servants called to minister. Humility does not require us to adopt a small mindset or a diminished opinion of ourselves, instead it is the weight that helps us keep our fleshly desires in check. Humility helps us to assess our internal opinions of ourselves with wisdom. This honest and open view of ourselves allows us to embrace self-care without guilt as it is an exercise of respecting ourselves, our physical and emotional needs, all while not seeking personal reward, acknowledgement, or glory. When exercising humility, we can see ourselves more clearly. It will then become more natural for us to care for ourselves out of genuine care for our own needs. To do this helps us avoid both pride and self-neglect.

We *can* understand our inherent worth and our need for

YHVH simultaneously, which provides the opportunity to care for ourselves in a way that is strengthening, rather that diminishing us and our ability to serve others and the special purpose that YHVH has placed in each one of us.

When we take it a step further, we can practice self-care as an act of gratitude and thankfulness and ultimately as an act of worship. Not worship of ourselves, but in the knowledge that when we care for our bodies, minds, and souls in reverence of the One that created us, no matter our limitations, we are honoring YHVH's choice to put us here. In Psalm 23 we see a beautiful picture of YHVH as a shepherd that provides rest, shelter, guidance and restoration to His flock. Self-care as worship becomes about caring for ourselves with mindfulness, embracing all He has provided for us as gifts directly from Him. Practices like observing His Sabbath, prayer, meditation on His Word, are not merely requirements. They are self-care activities that are also acts of obedience, devotion and celebration that remind us of the Great Shepherd's consideration, presence and provision in our lives. By viewing self-care as worship, we invite YHVH into all aspects of our lives, treating rest and renewal as acts that prepare and equip us to fulfill our calling and glorify and acknowledge Him in all we do.

> *"In all your ways acknowledge Him,*
> *and He will make your paths straight."*
> *Proverbs 3:6*

Personal Reflections:

1. How does the "overflow principle" of self-care encourage you to care for yourself so that you can more effectively care for others?
2. How do you maintain a balance between self-worth and humility? In what ways might humility enhance rather than detract from your sense of self-worth?
3. Reflect on the idea of self-care as worship. How can you view your daily self-care practices as ways to honor YHVH?
4. How does the perspective on YHVH's presence, through Sabbath and His set apart times, enhance your understanding of self-care as a spiritual practice? How might you incorporate these practices into your life to experience a deeper connection with YHVH?

BIBLICAL SELF-CARE
IN EVERYDAY LIFE

"Be still, and know that I am Elohim."
Psalm 46:10a

As we have explored, practicing self-care in alignment with Biblical teachings requires a new understanding or re-framing of our already established biases of what self-care is. Why is it that we can respect the needs of others, but ignore and disrespect our own needs? We are also YHVH's creation, and yet we do not extend that same care to ourselves. This becomes problematic when we consider that YHVH has required His people to be good stewards of all He has given ([1]Matthew 25:14-45, [2]1 Corinthians 4:2). Nowhere in His Word are we instructed to neglect ourselves and what He has given us to care for. And yet, this is our understanding.

If you're tired and burnt out, adding self-care to your day can just feel like the straw that broke the camel. Or, if you're an "all or nothing" person, it can become a sole focus and throw everything out of whack. But beginning a practice of self-care doesn't need to be dramatic or disruptive to your already busy life. Self-care can be present even in the simple choices in which you pause and give yourself permission to meet your own needs, no matter how small. Allowing yourself to enjoy simple pleasures, and engaging in activities that revitalize and encourage you can only enhance your life as you make room for yourself amongst the demands of daily living.

Just as YHVH provided rest and nourishment to Elijah when he'd had enough and found himself overwhelmed by Jezebel's mission to kill him ([3]1 Kings 19:1-6), YHVH provides opportunities for us to be restored. While the help He sends may not be as dramatic as sending an angel to feed and minister to us, He does provide these times for us if we are attentive.

Daily prayer and reflection are the perfect place to begin practicing self-care. Not only are they important to our relationship with YHVH, but both are a firm foundation for balanced self-care as they keep us connected to His presence and guidance. Through regular prayer, we invite Him to help us examine our hearts, and we teach ourselves how to embrace His love and guidance even as we grow in self-awareness and wisdom ([4]Psalm 139:23-24).

By establishing a daily routine of reflection, prayer, journaling, reading, and meditating on Scripture, we create an oasis of rest in which we will experience YHVH's presence, receive His peace, and allow His Word to shape our self-image. Remember, balance comes from grounding our identity in a sense of self that is rooted in YHVH's love for us.

"Keep your heart with all diligence, for out of it is the wellspring of life." Proverbs 4:23

Having boundaries is also a way in which we practice self-care and self-respect. Boundaries help us protect our hearts and minds from emotional and spiritual harm, allowing us to engage with others from a place of strength and integrity. Boundaries also free us from the burden of trying to fix things we aren't meant to, and prevents us from taking on the problems and responsibilities that belong to others.

Setting boundaries feels threatening and selfish at first if we aren't used to doing so, and likely the people in our lives will fight us as we try to establish boundaries where there haven't been any before. However, YHVH is all about boundaries. He sets boundaries all through Scripture, not just in Torah, but also in showing us what is His to take care of, and what is ours to take care of. By having good boundaries, we are practicing discernment and good stewardship of our time and resources. There is nothing wrong with being purposeful in how we distribute our energy and emotional investment within our relationships and responsibilities. Boundaries in relationships allow us the blessing of giving to others without neglecting our own well-being, ensuring that we can sustain a loving, healthy presence in our lives, families, and communities.

In Galatians [5]6:2, Paul instructs believers to *"bear one another's burdens,"* while later on in verse 5 he reminds us *"for each man will bear his own burden."* This may seem like double-speak, but it is a description of a balance that encourages us to support one another without taking on responsibilities that are not ours to carry. To a point, each person must maintain their own well-being.

While we do have the capacity to bear each other's burdens, it does depend on our own spiritual, emotional, and physical health. It also depends on our giftings and callings and what YHVH is asking of us in that moment. When we take care of ourselves properly, we are better able to respond to the needs of others with compassion, patience, and endurance. When we make ourselves a priority and learn to allow time to have our cup filled through self-care, we YHVH to fill us to overflowing during our time in prayer with Him. *Now* we can pour into others from a place of abundance rather than depletion, obligation, or fear. When we can do this, the experience of helping others becomes not only a blessing to those we minister to, but a blessing to ourselves, and the experience is much more joyful for the giver and the receiver.

Another powerful piece of self-care is practicing gratitude. Gratitude helps shape the way we perceive our lives, and strengthens a positive, YHVH-centered sense of self-worth. Paul also touches on this subject in Philippians 4:11-13, where he says, *"I know how to be humbled, and I also know how to abound. In any and all circumstances I have learned the secret both to be filled and to be hungry, both to abound and to be in need. I can do all things through Yeshua who strengthens me."* By cultivating gratitude in our lives, and keeping our eyes on YHVH and Yeshua, we learn to appreciate and see YHVH's provision, even in the times of hunger or need. This leads to a content and peaceful spirit that trusts itself in the very capable hands of the Creator.

Gratitude always combats negative self-perceptions, allowing us to take the focus from ourselves so we can see the many ways that YHVH blesses us and moves with quiet simplicity in our daily lives. Many times, He shows up without us noticing, but if we can see and praise Him for the smallest gifts He sends, we can appreciate everything fully. By having an attitude of thankfulness ([6]1 Thessalonians 5:18), we create joy in our lives, and it reminds us of how much our Father deeply loves us, even in the valleys.

Gratitude shifts our attention from what we perceive to be lacking and refocuses us on the blessings that are right before us. By practicing gratitude and thankfulness we also strengthen our relationship with YHVH, develop resilience, and nurture a healthy, balanced mind-set that is focused on rejoicing in YHVH's love and provision for us, His chosen people.

Personal Reflections:

1. Daily reflection and prayer are essential in our daily walk. What specific practices or routines could you establish to connect with YHVH and reinforce your sense of self-worth?

2. What boundaries might you need to set to *"guard your heart"* and protect your spiritual, emotional, and physical well-being? What small steps can you take to start setting those boundaries?

3. How does gratitude shape your view of self-love and contentment? In what ways can you practice gratitude to nurture a healthy perspective on life?

4. In what ways can self-care prepare you to serve others from a place of wholeness? How can you avoid burn-out while still fulfilling your responsibilities?

5. Are there some commitments or areas of your life that you need to let go of?

SELF-CARE AND THE
FRUITS OF THE SPIRIT

"But the fruit of the Spirit is love, joy, peace, patience, kindness, goodness,
faith, gentleness, and self-control.
Against such things there is no law."

Galatians 5:22-23

The Fruits of the Spirit are qualities that grow in our lives when we live in alignment with YHVH. These virtues are not only the markers of spiritual maturity, but also are part of living in freedom and having a fulfilling life. When applied to the discipline of self-care, these same fruits provide a guide for caring for our well-being while remaining rooted in our faith.

The Fruits of the Spirit reflect YHVH's character. By learning to cultivate them in our lives, we grow, produce fruit, which then allows us to sow seed and then reap a harvest. It is the same cycle that YHVH established in His calendar, and by learning to live in that pattern, we honor Him and reflect His character in our lives and to those around us.

Love

As we have talked about in several chapters, love serves as

the foundation for everything we do. Whether it is the presence of love, or the lack of love. It isn't a surprise that love is the first mentioned in Paul's list, as it is the foundation for all the other fruits to grow in our lives.

Love exists because YHVH is love. He created everything with love, and He made us with a great ability to love. Love is an invitation to see ourselves and others through YHVH's eyes, as His beloved creation, formed with His own hands, breathed into with His own breath/spirit. We are all born worthy of the love and consideration of our Creator, and as we have explored in the previous chapters, self-love and consideration is not selfishness when seen in the light of this truth.

Self-love and consideration are different for everyone, but practical ways we can love ourselves are by speaking kindly and compassionately to ourselves, avoiding harsh self-criticism and judgements. We can teach ourselves to appreciate our strengths, forgive our real or perceived weaknesses, and accept that YHVH's grace is sufficient for us.

Joy

Joy is a deep, abiding sense of delight in YHVH's presence and His blessings. True joy pours from a heart that is centered on Him, rather than circumstances. In self-care, joy and wonder can be present in our lives when we involve ourselves in activities that make us feel alive and connected with YHVH and His creation. Hiking, creative hobbies, making or listening to music are all great ways to spark joy in our lives.

Joy is the response of a thankful, content heart. Taking time to reflect on YHVH's blessings, and the reminders of YHVH's goodness and presence in our lives will help quiet the voice of doubt and negativity. Practicing gratitude and pausing to give thanks for all He has done for us brings joy to the forefront of our minds. Making time for laughter, connection, and fellowship with your loved ones and faith communities also creates joy, and joy-filled relationships nurture us through the good and the bad.

Peace

Peace is both a gift from YHVH, and a Fruit of His Spirit, offering calm and rest amidst life's challenges. YHVH's peace has the ability to guard our hearts and minds through difficult times if we learn to lean on Him and trust Him with the outcome. In the midst of the storm, it is important to find times of quiet so we can purposefully create space for stillness, reflection, and reliance on YHVH's strength.

In daily self-care, peace can be practiced by setting aside time for prayer and meditation on Scripture. You can create a physical prayer closet or other restful areas in your home or yard, where you can be free from unnecessary distractions. Remove the television from the bedroom. Turn off the phones at a certain time before bed. Set aside times in your day where you give yourself opportunities to disconnect and reset.

Patience

Patience is essential in self-care. It reminds us to honor the process of growth and healing. Ecclesiastes 3:1 reminds us *"For everything there is a season, and a time for every purpose under heaven."* Whether we are working on physical health, emotional healing, spiritual growth, or waiting for answers to our prayers and petitions, patience allows us to trust in YHVH's timing. It helps us remain steady as we work through whatever season we are in.

Self-compassion is important when we are exercising patience, because often, it is self-criticism or fear that leads us to act spontaneously or without wisdom. The truth is, the times we need patience are often the most uncomfortable seasons of our lives, so we want to rush through them. But we can't if we want to walk from that experience better than when we entered it. How we extend compassion to ourselves through those times, how we speak *to* and *of* ourselves in those seasons of growth, waiting, or grieving will influence our ability to just sit and be still as YHVH does His work within us (Philippians 1:6). He always provides a way and gives us strength and clarity while we are walking through the valleys.

Kindness

Kindness and goodness are part of YHVH's character and just as He extends those gifts to us, it is important to allow His treatment of us to extend to how we treat ourselves and others. Ephesians 4:32 encourages us to *"be kind to one another, tender hearted, and forgiving each other,"* which includes showing kindness and tenderness towards ourselves. Self-care rooted in kindness means making choices that support your health, balance, and spiritual well-being.

Show your body kindness by listening to it and not pushing it so hard. Make healthy choices as often as possible and within your means. Stay physically active, find ways to gently encourage yourself to create habits that support your physical and mental wellness.

Show your mind and emotions kindness by speaking well to yourself, not with arrogance, but with loving truth and compassion just as you would speak to someone you love going through the same situations and struggles. Take control of your mind and be aware of your self-talk. Speak life over yourself, using encouraging words instead of tearing yourself down. Speak YHVH's promises in Scripture over yourself and in response to thoughts that disagree with who He says you are. Use His word to affirm your identity in Yeshua and who YHVH says you are as His child.

Practice acts of self-kindness, treating yourself to something small after getting through a trying day, resting or taking a short nap before tackling a complex task or problem, enjoy your favorite hot beverage in the morning stillness before starting your day. Small acts of kindness toward yourself will go a long way in helping you navigate the stresses of life.

Faithfulness

Faithfulness involves being consistent and steadfast, even when challenges or doubts are present. Through faithfulness, we are able to stay committed to the practices of our faith in our daily life, as well as staying steadfast in our choice to practice self-care. Life is always going to be complex and fast paced. Situations will come along that are overwhelming. But staying committed to your choice to care for yourself will nurture the *entirety* of your being. Proverbs 3:5-6 reminds us to *"trust in Adonai with all your heart,"* and to acknowledge Him in all our ways. A good way to begin the self-care journey is to combine our self-care with the faithfulness of our faith walk.

When I began my self-care journey, combining my self-care practices (journaling, walking or sitting outdoors) with my faith practice helped relieve my mind of the guilt I felt for putting myself first. By combining my personal time with Scripture reading, meditating on the Word, listening to worship music, or praying, I was able to not only help myself stay steadfast to this new strange thing I was giving myself permission to experience, but I was also setting aside specific time to make YHVH a priority. By doing this, I found that I was able to stay not only faithful to YHVH, even as I was able to stay faithful to caring for myself despite feeling like I didn't deserve it or like my time could have been better used doing something for others instead of myself. It wasn't too long before I craved and missed that time if I didn't make it a priority, which helped me stay on track.

Finding practical ways to apply faithfulness to your own self-care routine can be finding spaces in your life where you can combine it with your self-care or finding small areas of time in your daily life that you can squeeze in a few moments to take care of your own rest and physical care. Set aside time to reflect on your spiritual journey and ask YHVH to guide your steps (Proverbs 16:9). Choose to stay faithful to the boundaries you have set in place that protect your time, energy, and peace.

Gentleness

Gentleness is *not* a weakness even though the world would like us to believe it is. Treating ourselves and others with tenderness and understanding is the same as Yeshua being gentle with us (Matthew 11:28-30). It is difficult sometimes not to be extremely critical of ourselves, but we need to learn to extend the same compassion and gentleness to ourselves as we do to the ones we love when we experience moments of failure or weakness.

Self-care rooted in gentleness allows us to slow down, give ourselves grace, and listen to our own needs with compassion. To be gentle with ourselves allows us to take care of ourselves without guilt and shame.

To exercise gentleness with yourself means resting when you are tired and resisting the urge to overextend and overcommit yourself. It involves speaking gently to yourself when you perceive that you are failing and speaking life-affirming Scriptural truths over yourself rather than beating yourself down with self-criticism. Practicing activities that you find relaxing or refreshing can also be ways that you can show gentleness to yourself.

Self-Control

The final Fruit of the Spirit is crucial in every area of our lives, and is associated with maturity, both spiritually and emotionally. Through self-control we temper ourselves and submit to YHVH's ways and purpose for our lives. Self-control is a crucial element for maintaining healthy habits and boundaries in life. It is also self-control that will help keep our flesh in check when it wants self-care to be strictly about pleasing itself.

Self-control keeps us steady, focused and empowered to make choices that honor YHVH and protect our well-being, which helps us avoid excess or neglect. In 1 Corinthians 9:25-27 Paul tells us how important self-control is in our lives,

> *"Every man who strives in the games exercises self-control in all things. Now they do it to receive a corruptible crown, but we an incorruptible. I therefore run like that, not aimlessly. I fight like that, not beating the air, but I beat my body and bring it into submission, lest by any means, after I have preached to others, I myself should be disqualified."*

Seeing self-control present in your life will look like setting boundaries over your time and energy to avoid burnout. It forces us to practice wisdom and discernment as the Spirit of YHVH teaches and guides us to avoid overindulgence, unhealthy habits and selfish behaviors. It helps us discipline ourselves and create consistency in our routines for spiritual, emotional, and physical health. It helps us assess and acknowledge our emotions, without making choices or having reactive behaviors based on what our emotions may be telling us about what is happening.

The Fruits of the Spirit provide a clear guide for self-care and the fruits YHVH wants to see us grow in every area of our lives. By applying love, joy, peace, patience, kindness, goodness, faithfulness, gentleness, and self-control in our daily lives, we learn to align ourselves, our self-care, and our decisions with YHVH's character. By obeying His framework for upright living, we are able to live in deeper relationship with Him, even as we nurture our well-being.

As we learn to cultivate these fruits in our lives or start to recognize them as they begin to grow as a result of our obedience and relationship with YHVH, remember that they are the work that YHVH has used His Spirit to do in you. And that [1]He is always faithful to complete any good work He begins in us if we are willing to partner with Him. Trust in His guidance, lean on His strength, and watch as He shapes your life into a beautiful testimony that honors and reflects His love!

Personal Reflections:

1. How can you show yourself love in a way that reflects YHVH's care for you?
2. Are there areas where you struggle to extend grace or compassion to yourself?
3. What brings you joy and draws you closer to YHVH's presence? How can you incorporate moments of joy into your self-care routine?
4. Where in your life do you most need YHVH's perfect shalom? How can you create space for rest and stillness in your daily routine?
5. Are there ways that you struggle with patience in your life? In what ways can you remind yourself to trust in YHVH's timing and process?
6. How can you show yourself kindness in your daily habits and routines? What does goodness look like in your approach to self-care? How can you use your self-talk to encourage and uplift yourself?
7. In what ways can you be more faithful to your decision to take better care of yourself? How does staying consistent in self-care deepen your trust and relationship with YHVH?
8. How can you approach yourself with gentleness during times of stress or difficulty? In what ways can you slow yourself down and listen to your own needs?
9. In what areas of your self-care routine do you struggle with self-control? How can practicing good discipline lead to greater balance and peace?

THE DISCIPLINE OF
A HEALTHY MIND

*"For though we walk in the flesh, we don't wage war according to the flesh;
for the weapons of our warfare are not of the flesh, but mighty before Elohim
to the throwing down of strongholds, throwing down imaginations and every
high thing that is exalted against the knowledge of Elohim and bringing
every thought into captivity to the obedience of Yeshua."*

2 Corinthians 10:3-5

Self-control is the cornerstone of a disciplined and YHVH-honoring life. While we explored it in the previous chapter, it is such a vital component to self-care that it deserves more attention. Self-care discussions often focus on physical or emotional well-being, Scripture shows us that the mind is the key to having a victorious life. Our thoughts influence the way we perceive ourselves and others. Our thoughts feed our emotions and resulting actions. When we learn to exercise self-control over our thoughts and train our minds to align with YHVH's truth, we protect our mental and spiritual health at the root.

Through self-control and learning to take every thought captive, we learn to renew and discipline our minds, which is a profound act of self-care that fosters resilience, clarity, and spiritual growth.

The thoughts that we allow ourselves to entertain are very powerful. In Proverbs 4:23 we are encouraged to *"keep your heart with all diligence."* In Biblical terms, the heart encompasses the mind, will, and emotions. To guard our thoughts is to be intentional not only about what we see and hear, but also about learning how to practice discernment, harness our self-talk, and challenge or discard wayward thoughts that the flesh and the enemy plant in our minds. Guarding our thoughts may be the most difficult, yet important exercise that we undertake in our spiritual walk. Challenging, but crucial to living a healthy, purposeful, and holy life.

Our thoughts shape how we view ourselves, the lens we see the world through and how we perceive others. Even more importantly, our thoughts shape how we perceive who YHVH is, and how we see or allow Him to move in our lives. When left unchecked, negative and harmful thoughts can lead to anxiety, fear, and self-doubt. On the other hand, thoughts rooted in YHVH's Word bring peace, joy, and confidence. Romans 12:2 encourages us to be *"transformed by the renewing of your mind,"* showing that our thoughts *must be aligned* with YHVH's truth in order for us to be transformed into the new creatures He intends us to be in Yeshua.

In [1]2 Corinthians 10:5, Paul is very clear that we must pay attention to our thoughts and bring them into submission to our obedience to Yeshua, who walked in Torah and was perfect ([2]Hebrews 4:15). To take our thoughts captive means recognizing negative or untrue thoughts, challenging them with Scripture, then discarding and surrendering them to YHVH. This discipline requires vigilance and intention, but we can teach ourselves to change our internal narrative by paying more attention to the things we are thinking and saying about ourselves and our lives. We can learn to combat fear, shame or inadequacy by replacing those negative things with YHVH's promises and prevent those things from taking hold in our hearts. We can combat fear with [3]Isaiah 41:10, we can rebuke shame with [4]Romans 8:1 and challenge the sense of inadequacy with [5]Philippians 4:13.

Actively challenging our thoughts will be exhausting at first, and it will feel like there is nothing safe to think about as we begin to take note of what thoughts we are entertaining. But by learning to control our thought life, we create a healthy, more YHVH-focused mindset, which will begin to trickle down through our emotional, physical and spiritual well-being.

By teaching ourselves self-control, we break down mental strongholds and learn to take responsibility for the management of our thoughts, emotions, and behaviors. This makes us mentally strong, and better able to resist the arrows of the enemy as our faith strengthens ([6]Ephesians 6:16). Self-control empowers us to resist temptations, avoid impulsive or emotional reactions, and focus on what aligns with YHVH's will and our self-care needs. Without self-control we are unable to establish or maintain healthy boundaries or create habits and routines that nurture our personal well-being.

Practicing self-control in our thought life involves being aware and present, along with identifying thought patterns, beliefs, and strings of thought that don't align with YHVH's truth. It teaches us discipline as we learn to redirect our thoughts to focus on prayer, Scripture, truth and gratitude. As we grow stronger through practicing self-control, the process becomes easier and more natural as we retrain ourselves. Through the process we gain greater peace and resilience, which equips us to face challenges with more grace and confidence than we would have as a frazzled mess of catastrophic thoughts.

In Philippians 4:6-8 we are encouraged to bring all our cares to YHVH and Paul tells us what types of thoughts we should entertain:

> *"In nothing be anxious, but in everything, by prayer and petition with thanksgiving, let your requests be known to יהוה. And the peace of יהוה, which surpasses all understanding, will guard your heart and thoughts in Messiah Yeshua. Finally, brothers, whatever things are true, whatever things are honorable, whatever things are just, whatever things are pure, whatever things are lovely, whatever things are of good report: if there is any virtue and if there is anything worthy of praise, think about these things."*

By allowing YHVH's Spirit to guide and transform our thoughts, and by focusing on Him we strengthen ourselves even more by filling our minds with His truth, His ways, and His purposes. Through this, we focus on the things of virtue and good report.

Part of self-control also involves setting boundaries around what we allow into our lives. The movies and other media we consume, the conversations we engage in, and the environments we frequent, all influence our thoughts and perceptions. While there is so much about life we can't control, we can control ourselves and many of the situations we put ourselves in. Even our friend groups can influence the path our lives take, as Proverbs 13:20 warns us:

> *"One who walks with wise men grows wise, but a companion of fools suffers harm."*

Choosing to surround ourselves with positive influences is the same as feeding our bodies healthy food, it helps us maintain our mental and emotional health and keeps our spirit-man strong.

Practical ways that we can protect our minds include limiting exposure to negative or harmful content on social media, news, or entertainment. It can also mean taking a break from those things or not taking part of them at all for some people. We can also make it a priority to have friendships with people that encourage, uplift, speak the truth in love, and influence us well, instead of placing ourselves in close relationships with those that manipulate, abuse, or influence us negatively. We can care for our minds and moods by regularly reading and studying Scripture, filling our minds with uplifting and YHVH-honoring music, sermons, podcasts, or books that inspire spiritual growth, or watching clean, wholesome entertainment.

By guarding what enters our minds, we create an environment that supports our decision to keep our thought lives healthy. While words like self-control and discipline often make us squirm uncomfortably, both bring us liberation. Though challenging, it is a profound action that radiates through every part of our lives. As we learn to put these concepts into practice, remember that YHVH's Spirit is at work in each of us, and that He tells us, *"...being confident in this very thing, that He who began a good work in you will complete it,"* (Philippians 1:6). If we take the steps needed to control ourselves according to YHVH's design, He will continue to work in and through us and help us to overcome in every area of our lives. Through prayer, meditation on His Word, and intentional boundaries, we can have a thought life that honors YHVH and reflects His love as we learn to walk in the full freedom of His grace.

Personal Reflections:

1. What thoughts tend to dominate your mind? Are they aligned with YHVH's truth? What are the roots of them?
2. How does guarding your mind and heart influence and change your emotional and spiritual health?
3. Are there recurring thoughts in your life that need to be taken captive? How can you counter them with Scripture? What practical steps can you take to make this practice a daily habit?
4. How does self-control help you care for your mind and spirit? In what areas of your life could you learn to practice greater self-control?
5. How can prayer and meditation help you align your thoughts with YHVH's truth and purpose? What verse or prayers might you use to combat harmful thought patterns?
6. Where can you make space in your day to meditate on a verse that challenges negative thought patterns?
7. What boundaries can you set to protect your mind from negative influences? How might your environment or relationships support or hinder your mental well-being?

REST, SOLITUDE,
AND THE SABBATH

*"If you turn away your foot from the Sabbath, from doing your
pleasure on My holy day,
and call the Sabbath a delight, and the holy of Adonai honorable
and honor it...then you will delight yourself in Adonai, and I will
make you to ride on the high places of the earth,
and I will feed you with the heritage of Jacob your father."*

Isaiah 58:13-14

The Sabbath is extremely important to YHVH. All
through His word He talks extensively about the
purpose of the Sabbath, and His expectations for His
people to observe it. It is the core of our faith practice and was
created and observed by YHVH at the beginning of creation
([1]Genesis 2:2-3). Rest is a practice that He has woven into our
very design, and it deeply affects our well-being.

In Scripture we can see numerous examples of how YHVH
values our physical, emotional, and spiritual health, the
foundations set up specifically in His Torah. He provides very
clear descriptions of how He expects us to care for ourselves.
From the keeping of the Sabbath, to boundaries, and proper care
for our bodies and spirits, He repeatedly reminds us that self-

care is both a responsibility and a gift from Him.

The first example and prominent instruction for self-care is the command to observe the Sabbath. In [2]Exodus 20:8-11, He commands the children of Israel and all the strangers among them to keep the Sabbath day set apart to Him. Not only is the Sabbath a *"sign and seal"* between YHVH and His people ([3]Exodus 31:112-17, [4]Ezekiel 20:12), it was set aside specifically as a period of time in which we are to rest and refresh ourselves. This set apart day is not only about physical rest, but also a special time for spiritual renewal and reconnection with YHVH. From the beginning, He an island of rest in which we are able to let go of our daily work responsibilities to refocus and worship Him. The Sabbath is also a wonderful time to strengthen our connections with friends, family, and our faith communities at large.

The Sabbath is the first illustration of a rhythm that YHVH built into creation, and it is the foundation for all the following set-apart times that He would describe to the children of Israel while He was teaching them in the wilderness. Yeshua further highlights the purpose for the Sabbath in Mark 2:27, *"The Sabbath was made for man, not man for the Sabbath."* Sabbath is a gift from YHVH to man, a time to nourish our minds, bodies, and spirits and is an invitation to practice self-care. It is a reminder that rest isn't optional, it's essential for not only our physical health, but also our spiritual health.

The Sabbath serves as a boundary, establishing a balance of work and rest. Anticipating it gives us something to look forward to during the week. We look forward to the blessing of rest, practices of prayer, family gatherings and communal worship, all of which rebalance us and help us walk into a new week with refreshed minds and bodies.

The stewardship of our bodies is also very important to YHVH. In [5]1 Corinthians 6:19-20, Paul teaches us that our bodies are temples of the Holy Spirit. We treat our spaces of worship as set apart, but Paul begs us to consider that our bodies should be cared for in the same way, with respect and care. The idea of caring for our bodies as a fit vessel for YHVH's Holy Spirit to move through and dwell in is a high honor reserved only for humanity. By caring for our physical person, we acknowledge that our lives and our bodies are a gift from Him, and that we have the honor of walking His ways and His purpose in our lives ([6]Proverbs 3:6).

Good stewardship of our bodies involves several things, proper nourishment, exercise, maintaining our health, good hygiene, rest, and keeping YHVH's instructions in Torah. Not only did He give us a gift that sets us apart as His people, but it is also about maintaining the health of His children so we can live abundantly! To keep the dietary laws (Leviticus 11) is to highlight respect for the body as part of our spiritual disciplines, and a reminder that what we consume impacts not only our physical health, but our spiritual health as well.

Paul encourages us to see our bodies as instruments for worship and service. In [7]Proverbs 3:7-8, wisdom is associated with health, so clearly caring for our bodies is not vanity or selfishness, it is how we stay strong and ready to serve YHVH. Paul's perspective encourages us to prioritize physical health as part of our spiritual discipline, which is a direct observance of Torah as much of it is centered around diet and cleanliness.

Throughout the Gospels, we see Yeshua setting boundaries and taking time for His own personal renewal. He frequently withdrew from the crowds that sought Him out for teaching and miracles. He purposefully removed Himself to pray and be alone, modelling a pattern of rest, reflection and reconnection with His Father. In [8]Mark 1:35, He rose early to pray, fueling Himself before His day began and the people sought Him out. We also see in Luke 5:16 that *"He withdrew himself to the desert and prayed."* Just like us, He needed to stay centered, replenished, and prepared so He could be a capable vessel for YHVH to work through.

By His example, self-care is an essential part of maintaining emotional and spiritual health. We already know that *"the spirit is indeed willing, but the flesh is weak"* (Matthew 26:41), and how much more do we weaken ourselves when we don't make caring for ourselves a priority? By seeking quiet times to listen for YHVH's voice, in solitude, and rest, we are able to strengthen our connection with Him and have a clearer mind and greater resilience in the chaos of life. We need to stop considering times of quiet and rest as "laziness" or "selfishness" and instead acknowledge that they are *necessary acts of renewal* that better equip us to live at peace with ourselves and others. Like the old proverb says, "you cannot pour from an empty cup", but we still see ourselves as required to do just that even though YHVH's Word says quite the opposite!

I believe that choosing rest and caring for our bodies is part of walking The Way as the Patriarchs and Yeshua did. Caring for our bodies as a vessel for His Spirit demonstrates reverence and obedience to His commandments and is a form of worship and acknowledgement of Him.

YHVH desires for us to live rooted in Him, with healthy and balanced lives. His commandments to rest on the Sabbath, being good stewards of all He has given us, and practicing healthy boundaries all combine to make us capable of living in His purpose. By living in the natural rhythm that He has given to us, we are better equipped to live in abundance, completely grounded in His love while being a spring of hope and life to those around us.

Personal Reflections:

1. How does observing Sabbath rest relate to your own well-being? What blessings do you experience by observing the Sabbath?

2. In [5]1 Corinthians 6:19-20, Paul describes the body as a *"temple of the Holy Spirit."* How does this perspective challenge or change your approach to caring for your physical health.

3. Yeshua often withdrew to pray and be alone ([8]Mark 1:35). Do you feel comfortable setting boundaries for solitude and renewal? Where and how can you create space in your life for prayer, rest, and reflection?

4. How might viewing self-care as an act of good stewardship change the way you approach your health, time, and resources?

EMOTIONAL HEALING
AND SELF-LOVE

Heal me, O Adonai, and I will be healed.
Save me, and I will be saved;
for You are my praise.

Jeremiah 17:14

Trauma leaves deep wounds on our hearts, minds, and bodies, shaping how we see ourselves, others, and even YHVH. These wounds, if left untended, can lead to deep-seated feelings of unworthiness, broken or dangerous relationships, and can limit us with fear and hypervigilance.

Healing from trauma is not easy, and like grief, it isn't linear. However, learning to allow YHVH to heal and use our experiences for His glory is essential to living in freedom and wholeness.

While many times our instinct is to wrap ourselves up in the pain of our past as a form of protecting ourselves from it ever happening again, we don't realize that by doing so we continue to allow those individuals or situations to have ownership of us. Often this will lead us to putting ourselves into dangerous situations where we repeat the patterns of our lives, and instead of protecting ourselves we find more abuse and more trauma at the hands of broken people we may not have entertained if we had been whole and healed.

Accepting that our triggers and the responsibility of healing is ours alone can feel like a backhand slap to the face. After all, it seems unfair that while we are not responsible for what happened to us, it is left to us to manage and heal the fallout. But taking responsibility for our healing is the most profound act of self-care and self-love we can extend to ourselves. Healing allows us to find better more productive ways to move beyond events that have hurt us so badly.

Trauma, no matter what the cause, affects every aspect of our being. It manifests in many ways in our lives; emotional pain, physical symptoms, sleeplessness, a sense of overwhelming guilt and shame, and fears of all kinds. It stunts our emotional growth and every relationship in our lives, including with ourselves.

David wasn't a stranger to pain, and his cry to YHVH in Psalm 34:18 tells us how YHVH sees those of us who have endured trauma. *"יהוה is near to those who have a broken heart and saves those who have a crushed spirit."* Trauma leaves us feeling destroyed, used, and unworthy of anything good, yet YHVH desires for us to experience healing and freedom from the pain of our pasts.

The pain of trauma is not something that we can simply, "let go of" or "get over" without *intentional* care. Acknowledging what has been taken from us, and the disfunction and effects of what happened is the first step in acceptance. Allowing ourselves to address and see the root causes of the pain rather than suppressing or ignoring it, gives us our power back, and removes us from the role of *victim* to *survivor*, then finally *cycle-breaker* and *overcomer*.

While YHVH is the ultimate source of healing, we also need

to take responsibility for our part in the process. Yeshua often asked those He healed to participate in their own recovery. In [1]John 5:5-9 He asks a man who had been paralyzed for 38 years, *"Do you want to be made well?"* Just like that man, we need to recognize that healing begins with a desire and willingness to act and save ourselves. Being a damsel or dude in distress just solidifies our victimhood in our own minds. Our Savior has already come, but we need to be willing to be healed, we need to be willing for Him to move.

By taking responsibility for our healing, we are acknowledging the need for change to take place in our life. We are recognizing that while what happened to us is out of our control, we are the ones who need to make the choice now. Even though it is a choice that we shouldn't have been forced to make in the first place. Once we decide to take that responsibility on, we are ready to seek help, we are ready to be brave in the face of memories and triggers. We become open to learning how to help ourselves as we engage in practices that help us recover from our wounds.

Taking responsibility for our own healing doesn't mean that we are shouldering the burden alone, but that we are open to growth, and that we are ready and willing to cooperate with YHVH's work in our lives. By taking this step, we affirm our self-worth and learn how to embrace and see the hope of a restored future and a life that isn't riddled with potholes and crippling pain.

For trauma survivors, forgiveness is often the most challenging and misunderstood aspect of the healing process, but it is a key aspect of healing. For many of us, as we discussed earlier, we have been raised to have an unhealthy view of what forgiveness is, and how complete it should be. What is crucial to understand is that forgiving others *does not* excuse their actions towards us. We don't even need to seek them out and offer them our forgiveness. Neither does forgiveness require us to have a lack of boundaries with people that have hurt us or have continued to hurt us. Forgiveness is not a "get out of jail free" card that allows others to continue to treat you terribly.

Often people use forgiveness as a bartering chip, rationalizing their behavior and then using our fears of not being forgiven by YHVH if we can't forgive ([2]Matthew 6:14-15), or as an excuse to continue to have footholds in our lives because we are supposed to *"forgive 70x7"* ([3]Matthew 18:21-22), or as a guilt trip because we are to *"forgive as Yeshua have forgiven us"* ([4]Colossians 3:12-13).

Instead, forgiveness is a *gift*. It is a gift that YHVH extends to us if we only just ask and receive it. It is our broken flesh that often leads humankind to use forgiveness as a weapon instead of what it is intended for. And that intended purpose is *freedom*.

By forgiving others in a Scriptural framework, we are giving up our right to revenge or eye for an eye for their wrongdoings against us. By forgiving, we release the poison that they planted in us through whatever wrong they've done and allows us to lay it at the throne and give YHVH the ability to heal us.

As we learn to forgive, we find ourselves able to let go of the emotional and spiritual weight of the pain, which opens the door to healing. While it is not a quick and simple, "one and done" process, choosing to forgive is a powerful act of self-love, and has absolutely nothing to do with those that have harmed us.

Healing from trauma is a very individualized journey, but it often requires outside help from professionals as you begin to address the physical, emotional, and spiritual aspects of recovery. YHVH often works through various means to bring about healing, as He knows what we need far more than we do. By leaning on Him it is possible to find liberation and freedom as we take practical and intentional steps towards a bright future where our traumas don't define us or influence our choices and reactions.

Seeking professional help from a counselor or therapist trained in trauma recovery is a wonderful step, and even though it is terrifying at first, finding a professional that has a strong faith background will be a wonderful person to guide you forward. Therapy provides a safe place and comprehensive tools that can help safely process emotions, build resilience, and help us learn new skills to replace the maladaptive survival mode survivors often find themselves trapped in.

During the healing process it is also very important to make self-care a priority. Dealing with flashbacks, big emotions, anxiety, fear, and the changes that healing brings will be physically and emotionally demanding and exhausting. It is important to listen to your body and mind so that you don't do damage to yourself as you process the trauma. A good therapist will help guide you through the process, and prioritizing rest and activities that bring joy, relaxation and emotional and physical regulation will be very important. By caring for your body and mind, you will be able to put your best foot forward as you fight for your life, which is *exactly* what you are doing by standing up and saying, "NO MORE!"

Finding a way to process your emotions is another way that you can exercise self-care in your healing journey. Journaling, creative writing, poetry, writing a memoir, dance, artwork and other forms of creative expression can be powerful tools as you work through your emotions.

Also recognizing that you are not alone, and there are people on similar healing journeys can make you feel less lonely in your healing. Talk to trusted friends, family members, or join a support or emotional recovery group. Often, the people that abused us also isolated us, so by choosing to no longer be isolated, we give less power to having our voices silenced.

And finally, don't forget YHVH in the process. I know sometimes it is difficult to quantify our faith and relationship with Him in the face of what happened to us. Especially in the case of religious abuse. After all, we know that He is all powerful, and it is likely that you feel that He could have changed it all or saved you from what happened. And maybe that is true. I know from my own trauma history, that while He could have changed everything and saved me from years of pain, abuse and neglect, that *He never left me*. He never abandoned me in those situations. He was always there, comforting me and encouraging me. He doesn't leave us in the storm. Sadly, many of us were subjected to parents that were ill-equipped to raise healthy children, and if we escaped that, life brought its own damage and challenges at some point in our lives. But YHVH is the Great Healer, His *business* is restoration and having great stories to come from great tragedy. We can take the power from the people that hurt us, and we can take the power from the adversary by allowing YHVH to turn our ashes into beauty ([5]Isaiah 61:1-3). We will be surprised at how YHVH will use us to bless and minister to others that are struggling in the darkness of trauma once we begin our unique journey to healing.

By learning to rest in YHVH's promises and trusting Him, we can learn to accept that some things, while out of our control and not in our best interest, can be used for His glory none-the-less if we are willing to partner with our Creator and allow Him to guide us to healing and rest in Him.

The goal of healing is *restoration* - and this is YHVH's specialty. His promise of restoration is woven through the entirety of Scripture. In Joel 2:25, He declares, *"I will restore to you the years that the swarming locust has eaten."* This is His *personal promise* that no matter what has been stolen from us, He will bring beauty and purpose from it if we allow Him to.

Healing doesn't mean forgetting or ignoring the past, but instead, it means teaching ourselves the skills and right-thinking that allow us to live in freedom *from* the past, find peace in our present, and have the hope of a blessed future. No matter where you are in your journey, allow yourself to embrace the hope of restoration, and choose to trust that YHVH is working all things out for your good ([6]Romans 8:28) and that what mankind has meant for evil, He can turn for good ([7]Genesis 50:20).

No matter what has happened to you, or the curses and negative words that have been spoken over you, I want you to know that you have deep value as a child of YHVH, and that He is just waiting for you to allow Him to move powerfully in this area of your life. By addressing the wounds of your past and embracing tools for recovery, you will position yourself to experience YHVH's transformative power as you allow Him to bring beauty from brokenness.

As you move forward, remember that healing is a journey, not a destination. Be patient with yourself, be kind and compassionate with yourself. Celebrate the small victories, even if all you can celebrate today is the fact that you are sitting up in bed. And always lean on YHVH when the road gets difficult. It is a lot of work, and it can seem daunting and never-ending, but you *can* experience the freedom and restoration that YHVH desires for you. Your healing is not just for *your* benefit – the chains of your past dropping from your body, mind, and spirit will be a beautiful testimony of YHVH's power and will be a *gift* to those who will witness your story of hope, strength, and renewal.

Fight on, fighter. And never give up.

Personal Reflections:

1. How has trauma affected your life, relationships, and faith? What things in your life have been limited or affected by trauma?

2. Are there areas in which you have felt "crushed in spirit" that need YHVH's healing touch?

3. How does Yeshua's question, *"Do you want to get well?"* settle in your spirit? Do you feel resistant, fearful, or are you ready to accept the call to experience His transformational healing? What steps do you personally need to take to take responsibility for your healing journey?

4. Are there people, including yourself, whom you need to forgive as part of your healing journey? How can forgiveness help you release the emotional burden that you carry from your past trauma? What hangups and fears do you have about allowing yourself to forgive in this area?

5. What tools or practices do you need to look into or begin to implement that can help you with your current needs for healing? How can you invite YHVH into your healing process through prayer and Scripture?

6. How does YHVH's promises of restoration encourage you in your healing journey? What does restoration look like to you, both spiritually and emotionally?

FORGIVENESS OF SELF AND OTHERS

"As far as the east is from the west, so far has He removed our transgressions from us." Psalm 103:12

Forgiveness is one of the most powerful and difficult acts of self-love and liberation. It requires us to confront our pain, release bitterness, and embrace the healing that YHVH offers us so generously.

Forgiveness is a difficult subject, because like self-care, it is a very misunderstood topic in the church. Putting things "under the blood" or saying words of forgiveness do not make everything better. Especially when you find yourself in situations out of your control, or are being hurt repeatedly in the same way, by the same person. And what about forgiveness of oneself? That can often be the most difficult forgiveness of all.

It is important to remember that forgiveness has many layers, and it is not merely a one-time action. It is an ongoing practice of surrendering past hurts and allowing YHVH's grace to shape our hearts and minds. There will be times, especially if you are dealing with trauma, that it will feel like you just keep circling back and revisiting the same wounds over and over again. Or, that you believe you have forgiven someone, but there is another layer, and another opportunity to release more of the pain.

I also would like to remind you, just in case you're being told otherwise, that YHVH's call to us to forgive others **doesn't mean** that you need to stay in the situation. Forgiveness **is not permission** to be abused. There is nothing wrong with forgiving and then *removing* yourself from the situation or person for a time or even permanently. Forgiveness is not about allowing yourself to be victimized or staying in dangerous situations. The purpose is to allow yourself to let go of the right for retaliation, your eye for an eye, and instead, trust YHVH to deal with things in His way, in His time.

Not only is forgiveness a gift that YHVH gives us when we repent and turn back to Him, it is a gift He has given us that allows us to release our burdens even more fully upon Him, and trust that He will make things right. It takes the weight from us and allows us to free our minds from the poison of bitterness and hatred, both which grow in the fertile ground of unforgiveness. It frees us from drinking the poison, all the while, expecting the person that hurt us to die or suffer ([1]loosely quoted from Saint Augustine). We are the only ones that suffer when we carry the burdens of unforgiveness and resentment.

When we refuse to, or are unable to forgive, we allow those situations and those people to continue to influence our minds, and the lens that we see life through. But through forgiveness, YHVH not only allows us to free others, but free ourselves as well. When we learn to forgive ourselves and others, we experience peace, emotional freedom, and spiritual clarity. For some of us, we even experience physical healing as a result of allowing ourselves to forgive. Forgiveness is at the very heart of a loving relationship with YHVH, ourselves, and others. Forgiving allows us to live fully in the present, instead of being bound to our pasts.

Forgiveness is a divine gift, extended to us by YHVH through His son, Yeshua. Forgiveness brings us freedom, joy, and a renewed sense of purpose. Furthermore, embracing forgiveness as an act of self-love also allows us to grow in YHVH's grace and prepares us to live with compassion and peace.

Forgiving ourselves is often the most challenging aspect of forgiveness. We are very quick to show compassion and understanding to others, but we can be terribly critical and harsh with ourselves. Holding onto guilt, regret, and shame only chains us to our sins and our real or perceived failures. Yet, YHVH's Word reminds us that His compassion and grace is boundless in [2]Psalm 103:8-14.

Just as YHVH is willing to forgive our shortcomings, He gives us the opportunity to extend the same grace to ourselves.

Self-forgiveness involves accepting our humanity and our flaws while recognizing that we are still deeply loved by our Creator! When we forgive ourselves, we open our hearts to healing and release the burdens of guilt and shame. This is a very powerful way to practice self-love and helps us to move forward with new purpose and self-compassion.

Self-forgiveness isn't about giving ourselves free passes, justifying, rationalizing or ignoring our mistakes. It is about acknowledging, learning, and then releasing the burden into YHVH's hands and asking Him to help us improve in that area of our lives.

Likewise, forgiving others is also an act that transforms us, freeing our hearts from the chains of bitterness, anger, and resentment. Yeshua emphasizes the importance of forgiving others in The Lord's Prayer and throughout all His teachings. In Matthew 6:14-15 He says:

> *"For if you forgive men their trespasses, your heavenly Father will also forgive you. But if you don't forgive men their trespasses, neither will your Father forgive your trespasses."*

Forgiveness is central to our relationship with YHVH. The plan of Salvation, and why He sent His Son to die for us, all are central to our belief and our relationship with Him. By forgiving others, we are reflecting His mercy and grace.

Forgiveness of others is not about excusing harmful or abusive behavior, or about pretending that our pain doesn't exist. But it is about releasing our right to hold onto resentment and choosing to live with a spirit of compassion and freedom. When we forgive, we release the hold that the pain has on us, which allows YHVH to move in and fill us with His peace and joy where the anger once resided. It allows us to breathe and release ourselves from emotional bondage. And allows Him to do a healing work in us so that our pain can be turned into something that can be used to minister and encourage others. If we can allow Him to help us in this area, we will learn how to restore our ability to love others with generous and open hearts.

Not only did Yeshua's teachings on forgiveness offer insight into the importance of it, but His acts of forgiveness are a model for us to live by. His interactions, parables, and personal example demonstrated that forgiveness is a central part of entering YHVH's kingdom. His willingness to forgive, even as He was being crucified speaks of the depth of His love for us. Even as He was suffering at the hands of those He came to save, His heart was still committed to showing mercy ([3]Luke 23:34).

When we choose to forgive, we choose freedom. By embracing YHVH's grace for ourselves and extending it to others, we create space for peace, love and joy. Forgiveness is not only a personal act, but a transformative process, that allows us to not only embrace our identities as YHVH's forgiven children, but as people who are able to forgive and repair relationships and heal divisions. Even divisions within ourselves.

We are capable of forgiveness, because we have received forgiveness that was not deserved first. When we extend compassion to ourselves, release and lay down the weight of guilt and shame that holds us back, we can see the result of what forgiveness does. As an act of self-love, forgiveness heals, liberates and renews our hearts. It helps us to walk in YHVH's love and move forward with confidence, compassion, and a deeper sense of empathy for others. Through forgiveness we can learn to live in peace and harmony as we reflect His mercy and grace to those around us. Though difficult, and something we may feel we circle around like the children of Israel did in the desert, through forgiveness, we are able to find a pathway to healing, freedom and experiencing the fullness of YHVH's love for every one of us.

Personal Reflections:

1. How does forgiving yourself reflect an understanding of YHVH's grace and love?
2. Are there areas where you struggle to forgive yourself? If so, why?
3. In what ways does holding onto resentment or bitterness affect your emotion, spiritual and physical well-being?
4. How might forgiving yourself and others bring a sense of freedom and peace to your life? What steps can you take that will enable you to experience greater self-love and YHVH's peace?
5. How can Yeshua's example of forgiveness influence your journey to forgiveness and your sense of inner peace?

THE OUTPOURING
OF SELF-CARE

"So then, as we have opportunity, let's do what is good toward all men, and especially toward those who are of the household of the faith."

Galatians 6:10

S elf-care is not only an individual pursuit, but a holistic practice in which spiritual, emotional, and physical well-being are understood within the context of obedience and connection to YHVH. Through this approach, as we have seen, by caring for ourselves we are then capable of serving others and honor YHVH's commandments more fully.

As we reframe our concept of healthy, balanced self-care into more than selfish indulgence, and see it as an essential and beneficial element of living a balanced life it deepens the practices of prayer, Sabbath observance, and even the relationships and efforts that we make in our faith community.

The concept of community, [1]*kehilah*, is an important part of Jewish and Messianic life. In Hebrews 10:24-25, we are advised:

"Let's consider how to provoke one another to love and good works, not forsaking our own assembling together, as the custom

of some is, but exhorting one another, and so much the more as you see the Day approaching."

In the natural, we understand that there is strength in numbers. The march on Jericho, and also Yeshua's words in Matthew 18:20, support this concept of community and obedience being a necessary part of walking in His ways:

"For where two or three are gathered together in My Name, there I am in the middle of them."

Both the Torah and the New Testament encourage us to build strong, loving communities where individuals can grow ([2]iron sharpens iron – Proverbs 27:17), and support one another emotionally, spiritually, and physically.

Psalm 133 highlights the joy of the Body of YHVH coming together:

"See how good and pleasant it is
for brothers to live together in unity!
It is like the precious oil on the head,
that ran down on the beard,
even Aaron's beard,
that came down on the edge of his robes,
like the dew of Hermon,
that comes down the hill of Zion;
for there Adonai gives the blessing,
even life forever more.

While unity obviously encompasses shared belief, and celebration of tradition and family, it can also take the form of mutual support, with each member walking in their calling, and being a contributing member that supports other members of the Body ([3]Hebrews 10:24).

This begs the question, how are we able to care for others, if we do not first care for ourselves? What comes to mind is, how the older women are to teach the younger ([4]Titus 2:1-8). If we are not taking care of our homes properly first, how are we capable of leading, teaching, or influencing others by our example? Another example would be the instructions YHVH gave for who could serve the Nation of Israel as elders. They had to have their house in order before they could lead ([5]1 Timothy 3:4-5). While perfection is impossible and never required, it stands to reason that there is an expectation of leading by example in order to impact those around us.

While at times there will be a need for us to be supported by our faith community, whether it be through prayer, acts of service, or financial support, this does not mean that it is a weakness. Sometimes learning to ask for help and learning to accept it is an exercise of self-care. The Body has always been meant to be a type of extended family, and all of us, pieces of a whole that make it function properly. If we can create habits of self-care and self-control in our personal lives, this can spread to those in our study groups or assemblies as the community grows together through worshipping and studying together. As a by-product, fellowship and friendships built will provide emotional and spiritual nourishment. Thus, self-care spills over into a culture of love for community, with the energy to sow into it instead of being drained by it.

This unity allows us to share in each other's burdens and joys, which fulfills YHVH's call to care for each other.

The concept of [6]*teshuvah*, or repentance, which is a requirement for us to walk in Yeshua's footsteps, can also be seen as an act of self-care. After all, to turn away from sin is to choose to care for oneself and the impact that we have on those around us. *Teshuvah* provides a pathway to healing and renewal, to heal from both wounds we have inflicted on ourselves but also provides the way to make things right with others.

Teshuvah involves "turning away" from what is wrong, and turning back to YHVH, seeking forgiveness, and restoring our relationship with Him and others. Psalms 51:10 so beautifully says, *"Create in me a clean heart, O Adonai. Renew a right spirit within me."* Through *teshuvah*, we are able to experience the release of guilt and shame for our past actions and find the joy of being restored to YHVH. This healing strengthens our sense of self-worth, restores or aligns us with our core values, and enables us to make a fresh start. We are all prodigal children, and the importance of *teshuvah* cannot be ignored, from the large case of returning as the prodigal son did (⁷Luke 15:11-32), or the simple act of turning from sins that YHVH's Spirit reveals to us along the way.

True repentance is never made from religious duty; it is always from the cry of a broken heart that has reached the bottom. *Teshuvah* is a form of spiritual self-care. We do this every year as we observe Rosh Hashanah and reflect during the Days of Awe in preparation for Yom Kippur. This time allows us to engage in deep and honest introspection, ask for forgiveness for wrongs done, and forgive others. YHVH gives us this time to realign ourselves with Him and His will, so that He can hear our prayers, and move freely in the lives of willing vessels. Through this appointed time, we are also able to deepen our self-understanding and draw closer to YHVH as we embrace self-love that is grounded in humility, growth, gratitude, and restoration with our Creator, ourselves, and others.

> *"Come now, and let's reason together," says Adonai: "Though your sins are as scarlet, they shall be white as snow. Though they are red like crimson, they shall be as wool." Isaiah 1:18*

The entire process of *teshuvah* encourages self-love and self-compassion through the acceptance of YHVH's forgiveness and mercy for His children. By acknowledging our imperfections and allowing ourselves to be vulnerable and accountable to Him (because we already are, whether our hearts are softened to Him or not), we are able to embrace self-love that is free from condemnation and secure in our transformed identity in Yeshua.

YHVH's feasts and festivals, provide many structured opportunities for self-care, rest and spiritual reflection. The annual cycle of festivals, from Passover to Sukkot, can be so much more than traditional observances if we allow ourselves to fully enter in. It's a special invitation from YHVH to His people to enter into a cycle of celebration, repentance, and renewal, with each feast addressing different aspects of spiritual and personal growth that are essential for an abundant life in YHVH.

Rosh Hashanah provides a time of self-reflection, where we can assess our actions over the past year and seek to realign ourselves with YHVH's will and call on our lives. This season is focused on introspection and personal growth, renewing our commitment to an upright life.

Yom Kippur is a time of fasting and repentance where we examine ourselves in prayer and hold ourselves accountable for wrongs done to others and YHVH. It is a practice of purity and enables us to process and release the weight of our past sins and start fresh with a clean and renewed heart. We are commanded to afflict our souls, and fast, which serves as both a spiritual purification, exercise of self-control, and a reminder of our reliance on YHVH.

Sukkot is a joyful celebration of YHVH's provision and protection, encouraging believers to dwell in temporary booths to remember YHVH's faithfulness, strength and provision as He delivered us from Egypt. While we may not have personally walked with Moses out of Egypt, we all have our own personal version of Egypt in our lives that He has delivered us from. The act of dwelling in booths reminds us to walk in gratitude, humility, and contentment, all qualities essential for growth.

Every feast creates a unique space for us to pause, reflect, reset and remove ourselves from the mundane temporary things of this world, and refocus ourselves on YHVH's sovereignty and provision in our lives. The feasts are also times to reconnect us with our community as we celebrate all YHVH has done for us. Through observing the feasts and festivals, we are practicing self-care even while being obedient and practicing self-control, which keeps us grounded, thankful and open to hear YHVH's voice.

> *"Search me, Adonai, and know my heart. Try me, and know my thoughts. See if there is any wicked way in me, and lead me in the everlasting way." Psalm 139:23-24*

Prayer and meditation are also acts of self-care. Both create connection and intimacy with YHVH, that sustains us as we walk through a hurting and sinful world. In the [8]*Shema* ([9]Deuteronomy 6:4-9, [10]Numbers 15:37-41), we are commanded to love YHVH with all our heart, soul, and strength. This prayer is said as a daily reminder of devotion, declaration of YHVH's sovereignty, and helps us center our thoughts on YHVH's commandments and His presence in our lives.

Daily prayer not only keeps us connected to YHVH, but it also provides us with the opportunity to be intentional about setting aside quiet times when we can refuel and hear His voice. It is rare that we are capable of hearing Him over the chaos if we don't set aside personal time with Him, for His voice is still and quiet.

> *He said, [to Elijah] "Go out and stand on the mountain before Adonai." Behold, Adonai passed by, and a great and strong wind tore the mountains and broke in pieces the rocks before Adonai; but Adonai was not in the wind. After the wind there*

was an earthquake; but Adonai was not in the earthquake.
After the earthquake a fire passed; but Adonai was not in the
fire. After the fire, there was a still small voice.
1 Kings 19:11-12

The purpose of our creation has always been about connection with YHVH, and while we cannot walk with Him in the same way Adam and Eve did, He still provides His Spirit and yearns for us to approach His throne with our prayers and petitions. He desires a close relationship with all of us, just as a parent yearns for the hearts of their children. Through prayer and time in YHVH's Word, we find strength, comfort, and clarity. We find relationship and connection with our Creator, and it is there that is where our spirits are nurtured and our faith is strengthened.

Personal Reflections:

1. As we discussed, *kehillah* or community is a large part of self-care. Not just in giving to our community, but also in receiving support from our community. How does your faith community support your spiritual and emotional health?

2. What role does *teshuvah* play in your own journey of self-love? How does forgiveness-of yourself and others-contribute to your personal healing?

3. How do the Feasts, Festivals, and Sabbaths encourage practices of self-reflection and renewal? Are there certain seasons or days in your life where you are intentional about practicing reflection and connection with YHVH?

4. How does viewing self-care within a communal and relational context change your understanding of personal growth and healing?

CREATIVITY AND
SELF-CARE

*"Elohim created man in His own image. In Elohim's image He created
him; male and female He created them."*

Genesis 1:27

Creativity is a beautiful gift that reflects the image of our
Creator within us. YHVH showed His *boundless*
creativity in forming the world, shaping humanity from
clay, and weaving intricate beauty and purpose into every detail
of existence. When we engage in creative expression, especially
expressions that we dedicate to Him and furthering His
kingdom, we mirror this aspect of His creative nature. Through
creativity, we often find joy, healing, the ability to process our
emotions. We discover connection with YHVH and others in
the process. Creativity, in this sense, is not about producing, so
much as it is a part of self-care that nurtures our souls, allows us
to express ourselves, and allows us to experience YHVH's
presence in a deeply personal way.

By embracing creative practices, even something as simple as
daily journal writing or prayer and Bible journalling, we open
ourselves to renewal and spiritual growth, allowing YHVH's
beauty and purpose to flow through us.

I love how YHVH's story begins in Genesis 1 with a vivid

display of His creativity as He *speaks* everything of creation into existence! What an amazing description of His power, that just words from His mouth can create so much with so many intricacies, and everything being connected and in perfect harmony with the other.

Creativity easily becomes an act of worship when approached with a heart that honors YHVH. Whether through music, writing, or creative problem-solving, engaging in creative activities allows us to *celebrate* the gifts He has placed in us. Our gifts then become not just for others, but also a gift from Him to us. When we allow ourselves to create within His boundaries, we step into a space of freedom and joy.

Creative activities are also a powerful way to process emotions, release stress, find peace, and heal. The Psalms offer an example of how creativity through poetry and music was used by David to express his deepest emotions. In Psalm 42:5, David writes,

> *"Why are you in despair, my soul? Why are you disturbed within me? Hope in Adonai! For I shall still praise Him for the saving help of His presence."*

There are countless examples all through David's writings of how he used creativity to process and express his feelings, while at the same time, centering his gaze and his hope on YHVH. And through his creativity, YHVH used him to prophesy of the Messiah to come!

Our traditions offer numerous opportunities for creativity and celebration. The observance of feasts, such as Passover and Sukkot and the festivals of Hannukah and Purim involve creative storytelling, song, and decorations that honor and celebrate YHVH's commandments and hand of deliverance. For example, during Sukkot, believers construct and decorate booths, and during Purim we dress up and tell the tale of Esther.

During these celebrations we create a physical and artistic representation of YHVH's protection and provision and allow us to keep our traditions alive for future generations.

These traditions reflect the importance of creativity in fostering spiritual connection and joy with both YHVH and our family in Messiah. By engaging in acts of creativity, we can celebrate the interplay of beauty, worship, family, and community. Whether through cooking for the holy days, or leading music for corporal worship, these practices demonstrate how creativity can be a central part of self-care and spiritual renewal.

Integrating creativity into self-care routines does not require artistic mastery; it simply requires an openness to explore and express. There are simple ways to introduce creativity into your life:

Journaling - Reflect on your emotions and your day. Keep a gratitude or prayer journal. Create a War Binder or begin Bible Journaling.

Art - Painting, hand lettering, crafting, knitting/crochet as a way to relax and express yourself.

Music - Play an instrument, sing, or listen to music that uplifts and inspires you.

Storytelling - Creative writing, poetry and other forms of written expression can help you process experiences or express your thoughts.

Cooking or Baking - Making food not only nourishes the body but feeds the hearts of our families and community. Making meals for ourselves and others allows us to nurture and can also be a creative outlet where you can explore new recipes or techniques.

Nature Activities - Engage in photography, gardening, natural foods/foraging, learning about nature and other outdoor activities to appreciate YHVH and all He has created for us to care for and enjoy.

These examples are just a few of the ways we can allow ourselves time for personal reflection, quiet time with YHVH, moments of joy, and emotional release and regulation.

Creativity is a special gift that reflects the image of YHVH within us. By engaging in creative expressions, we nurture ourselves, find internal quiet, and reconnect with our Creator. Whether through music, writing, or our traditions, creativity provides a powerful pathway to healing and renewal that often spills over into the world when we begin to share the fruits of our creative endeavors.

As an act of self-care, creativity invites us to rest, play, reflect, and celebrate the unique gifts and purpose that YHVH has placed within us. By making room for creativity in our daily lives, we can deepen our sense of self-love and experience transformation in powerful and unexpected ways. Embracing creativity allows us to honor our Creator, partner with Him, and rediscover our inner strength even as we find peace in the natural rhythm of His creation!

Personal Reflections:

1. How does engaging in creative expression remind you of being made in YHVH's image?
2. What forms of creativity bring you the most joy and peace?
3. In what ways can creativity help you process emotions and challenges?
4. How might engaging in creative practices bring healing to areas in our life that feel like heavy burdens or unresolved?
5. What activities allow you to experience YHVH's beauty and presence in creative ways?
6. How do creative traditions, such as decorating for feasts and festivals, and preparing for Sabbaths enhance your spiritual connection? Are there ways you can bring creative expression into your worship or observances?
7. Which creative practices resonate the most with your interests and needs? How can you make space for regular creative activities as part of your self-care routine?

.

AFTERWARD

In a world that often promotes self-care as an end to itself, an escape from responsibility, or in a way that can quickly become unbalanced, my prayer is that this study has revealed a more well-rounded, Scriptural view in which self-care is seen both as a gift and act of reverence toward YHVH. By embracing self-love and self-care that is rooted in our identity as new creatures in Messiah, we nurture our well-being and better equip ourselves to be servants to the Most High.

As we learn to integrate this idea of balanced self-care into our lives, we will come to understand that self-care is a spiritual discipline that prepares us to fulfill our calling. Each act of self-care and self-compassion becomes an opportunity to fill ourselves from the source of our existence, for in Him we live, move, and have our being ([1]Acts 17:28). We are YHVH's creation, He tells us continually of His great love for us, and we were made with a purpose and for His glory.

Moving forward, never forget that true self-care is not a retreat from our responsibilities but is a gift that allows us to give from the same abundance that YHVH has given to us! By grounding our self-love in YHVH's truth, we can have lives of balance, resilience, and purpose. By nurturing our well-being and being good stewards of all we have been blessed with, we can reflect YHVH's light to the world as willing vessels of His love, fully equipped to bear the fruits of His Spirit as we carry His light into a very dark and starving world.

As you continue this journey, may you embrace the calling and purpose YHVH has in store for you! May you learn to balance self-love and self-care and find a life of freedom, abundance and wholeness. May you find peace in knowing that in caring for yourself, you are not only fulfilling YHVH's commandments but also preparing your heart to reflect His love abundantly in all that you do!

SCRIPTURE REFERENCES

Chapter One: Diagnosing Sickness

[1]Genesis 1:26-27 Elohim said, "Let's make man in our image,
after our likeness. Let them have dominion over the fish of the
sea, and over the birds of the sky, and over the livestock, and
over all the earth, and over every creeping thing that creeps on
the earth." Elohim created man in His own image. In Elohim's
image He created him; male and female He created them.

[2]Leviticus 19:18 "You shall not take vengeance, nor bear any
grudge against the children of your people; but you shall love
your neighbor as yourself. I am יהוה.

[3]Matthew 22:39 A second likewise is this, 'You shall love your
neighbor as yourself'.

[4]1 John 4:7-8 Beloved, let's love one another, for love is of יהוה;
and everyone who loves has been born of יהוה and knows יהוה.

Chapter Two: Reframing the Foundation

[1]Leviticus 19:18 "You shall not take vengeance, nor bear any
grudge against the children of your people; but you shall love
your neighbor as yourself. I am יהוה."

[2]Matthew 22:39 A second likewise is this, 'You shall love your
neighbor as yourself'.

³Genesis 2:7 Elohim formed man from the dust of the ground, and breathed into his nostrils the breath of life; and man became a living soul.

⁴1 Corinthians 12:12-26 For as the body is one and has many members, and all the members of the body, being many, are one body; so also is Messiah. For in one Spirit we were all baptized into one body, whether Jews or Greeks, whether bond or free; and we all given to drink in one Spirit.

For the body is not one member, but many. If the foot would say, "Because I am not the hand, I'm not part of the body," it is not therefore not part of the body. If the ear would say, "Because I'm not an eye, I'm not part of the body," it's not therefore not part of the body. If the whole body were an eye, where would the hearing be? If the whole were hearing, where would the smelling be? But now יהוה has set the members, each one of them, in the body, just as He desired. If they were all one member, where would the body be? But now they are many members, but one body. The eye can't tell the hand, "I have no need for you," or again the head to the feet, "I have no need for you." No, much rather, those members of the body which seem to be weaker are necessary. Those parts of the body which we think to be less honorable, on those we bestow more abundant honor, and our unpresentable parts have more abundant modesty, while our presentable parts have no such need. But יהוה composed the body together, giving more abundant honor to the inferior part, and there should be no division in the body, but that the members should have the same care for one another. When one member suffers, all the members suffer with it. When one member is honored, all the members rejoice with it.

[5]*Echad* (Strongs # 259) appears over 900 times in the Old Testament. In Hebrew echad is used to signify the concept of being united, oneness, first, and alone. Adam and Eve became one (echad) flesh – Elohim is one (echad). The root word is achad (Strongs #258), meaning to unify or collect.

[6]Psalms 8:3-5
When I consider Your heavens, the work of Your fingers,
the moon and the stars, which you have ordained,
what is man, that You think of him?
What is the son of man, that You care for him?

[7]Romans 3:23 For all have sinned, and fall short of the glory of יהוה.

[8]Philippians 4:7 And the peace of יהוה, which surpasses all understanding, will guard your hearts and your thoughts in Messiah Yeshua.

[9]Deuteronomy 6:4-5 Hear, Israel: יהוה is our Elohim, Elohim is one [*echad*]. You shall love יהוה your Elohim with all your heart, with all your soul, and with all your might.

[10]Ephesians 4:22-24 That you put away, as concerning your former way of life, the old man that grows corrupt after the lusts of deceit, and that you be renewed in the spirit of your mind, and put on the new man, who in the likeness of Elohim has been created in righteousness and holiness of truth.

[11]2 Corinthians 5:17 Therefore if anyone is in Messiah, he is a new creation. The old things have passed away. Behold, all things have become new.

Chapter Three: Balancing Love for Self and Others

[1]Deuteronomy 6:5 You shall love יהוה your Elohim with all your heart, with all your soul, and with all your might.

[2]Leviticus 19:18 You shall not take vengeance, nor bear any grudge again the children of your people; but you shall love your neighbor as yourself. I am יהוה.

[3]Mark 1:35 Early in the morning, while it was still dark, He rose up and went out, and departed into a deserted place, and prayed there.

[4]Matthew 14:23 After He had sent the multitude away, He went up into the mountain by Himself to pray. When evening had come, He was there alone.

[5]Matthew 16:24-25 Then Yeshua said to His disciples, "If anyone desires to come after Me, let him deny himself, take up his cross, and follow Me. For whoever desires to save his life will lose it, and whoever will lose his life for My sake will find it.

[6]Luke 10:25-37 Behold, a certain lawyer stood up and tested him, saying, "Rabbi, what shall I do to inherit eternal life?"

He said to him, "what is written in the Torah? How do you read it?"

He answered, "You shall love יהוה your Elohim with all your heart, with all your soul, with all your strength, and with all your mind; and your neighbor as yourself."

He said to him, "You have answered correctly. Do this, and you will live.

But he, desiring to justify himself, asked Yeshua, "Who is my neighbor?"

Yeshua answered, "A certain man was going down from Jerusalem to Jericho, and he fell among robbers, who both stripped him and beat him, and departed, leaving him half dead. By chance a certain priest was going down that way. When he saw him, he passed by on the other side. In the same way a Levite also, when he came to the place and saw him, passed by on the other side. But a certain Samaritan, as he traveled, came where he was. When he saw him, he was moved with compassion, came to him, and bound up his wounds, pouring on oil and wine. He set him on his own animal, brought him to an inn, and took care of him. On the next day, when he departed, he took out two denarii, gave them to the host, and said to him, 'Take care of him. Whatever you spend beyond that, I will repay you when I return.' Now which of these three do you think seemed to be a neighbor to him who fell among the robbers?"

He said, "He who showed mercy on him."

Then Yeshua said to him, "Go and do likewise."

[7]John 13:34-35 A new commandment I give to you, that you love one another. Just as I have loved you, you also love one another. By this everyone will know that you are My disciples, if you have love for one another.

[8]Matthew 5:14 "You are the light of the world. A city located on a hill can't be hidden. Neither do you light a lamp and put it under a measuring basket, but on a stand; and it shines to all who are in the house. Even so, let your light shine before men, that they may see your good works and glorify your Father who is in heaven."

[9]Philippians 2:1-4 If therefore there is any exhortation in Messiah, if any consolation of love, if any fellowship of the Spirit, if any tender mercies and compassion, make my joy full by being like-minded, having the same love, being of one accord, of one mind; doing nothing through rivalry or through conceit, but

in humility, each counting others better than himself; each of you not just looking to his own things, but each of you also to the things of others.

Chapter Four: Loving Others and Glorifying YHVH

[1]Romans 12:3 For I say through the grace that was given me, to everyone who is among you, not to think of yourself more highly than you ought to think; but to think reasonably, as יהוה has apportioned to each person a measure of faith.

Chapter Five: Biblical Self-Care in Everyday Life

[1]Matthew 25:14-45 "For it is like a man going into another country, who called his own servants and entrusted his goods to them. To one he gave five talents, to another two, to another one, to each according to his own ability. Then he went on his journey. Immediately he who received the five talents went and traded with them, and made another five talents. In the same way, he also who got the two gained another two. But he who received the one talent went away and dug in the earth and hid his master's money.

Now after a long time the master of those servants came, and settled accounts with them. He who received the five talents came and brought another five talents, saying, 'Master, you delivered me five talents. Behold, I have gained another five talents in addition to them.'

His master said to him, 'Well done, good and faithful servant. You have been faithful over a few things, I will set you over many things. Enter into the joy of your master.'

He also who got the two talents came and said, 'Master, you delivered to me two talents. Behold, I have gained another two talents in addition to them.'

His master said to him, 'Well done, good and faithful servant.

You have been faithful over a few things. I will set you over many things. Enter into the joy of your master.'

He also who had received the one talent came and said, 'Master, I knew you that you are a hard man, reaping where you didn't sow, and gathering where you didn't scatter. I was afraid, and went away and hid your talent in the earth. Behold, you have what is yours.'

But his master answered him, 'You wicked and slothful servant. You knew that I reap where I didn't sow, and gather where I didn't scatter. You ought therefore to have deposited my money with the bankers, and at my coming I should have received back my own with interest. Take away therefore the talents from him and give it to him who has the ten talents. For to everyone who has will be given, and he will have abundance, but form him who doesn't have, even that which he has will be taken away. Throw out the unprofitable servant into the outer darkness, where there will be weeping and gnashing of teeth.'

"But when the Son of Man comes in His glory, and all the holy angels with Him, then He will sit on the throne of His glory. Before Him all the nations will be gathered, and He will separate them one from another, as a shepherd separates the sheet from the goats. He will set the sheep on His right hand, but the goats on the left. Then the King will tell those on His right hand, 'Come, blessed of My Father, inherit the Kingdom prepared for you from the foundation of the world; for I was hungry and you gave Me food to eat. I was thirsty and you gave Me drink. I was a stranger and you took Me in. I was naked and you clothed Me. I was sick and you visited Me. I was in prison and you came to Me.'

Then the righteous will answer Him, saying, 'Master, when did we see You go hungry and feed You, or thirsty and give You drink? When did we see You as a stranger and take You in, or naked and clothe You? When did we see You sick or in prison and come to You?'

The King will answer them, 'Most certainly I tell you, because you did it to the one of the least of these My brothers, you did it to Me.' Then He will say also to those on the left hand, 'Depart from Me, you cursed, into the eternal fire which is prepared for the devil and his angels; for I was hungry, and you didn't give Me food to eat; I was thirsty, and you gave Me no drink; I was a stranger, and you didn't take Me in; naked, and you didn't clothe Me; sick, and in prison, and you didn't visit Me.'

Then they will also answer, saying, 'Master, when did we see you hungry, or thirsty, or a stranger, or naked, or in prison, and didn't help you?'

Then He will answer them, saying, 'Most certainly I tell you, because you didn't do it to on of the least of these, you didn't do it to Me.; These will go away into eternal punishment, but the righteous into eternal life."

²1 Corinthians 4:1-2 So let a man think of us as Messiah's servants and stewards of יהוה's mysteries. Here, moreover, it is required of stewards that they be found faithful.

³1 Kings 19:1-6 Ahab told Jezebel all that Elijah had done, and how he had killed all the prophets with the sword. Then Jezebel sent a messenger to Elijah, saying, "So let the gods do to me, and more also, if I don't make your life as the life of one of them by tomorrow about this time!"
When he saw that, he arose and ran for his life, and came to Beersheba, which belongs to Judah, and left his servant there. But he himself went a day's journey into the wilderness, and came and sat down under a juniper tree. Then he requested for himself that he might die, and said, "it is enough. Now, O יהוה, take away my life; for I am not better than my fathers."
He lay down and slept under a juniper tree; and behold, an angel

touched him, and said to him, "Arise and eat!"
He looked, and behold, there was at his head a cake baked on
the coals, and a jar of water. He ate and drank, and lay down
again. יהוה's angel came again the second time, and touched him,
and said, "Arise and eat, because the journey is too great for you.
He arose, ate and drank, and went in the strength of that food
forty days and forty nights to Horeb, יהוה's Mountain.

[4]Psalms 139:23-24
Search me, Adonai, and know my heart.
Try me, and know my thoughts.
See if there is any wicked way in me,
and lead me in the everlasting way.

[5]Galatians 6:2-5 Bear one another's burdens, and so fulfill the
Torah of Messiah. For if a man thinks himself to be something
when he is nothing, he deceives himself. But let each man
examine his own work, and then he will have reason to boast in
himself, and not in someone else. For each man will bear his
own burden.

[6]1 Thessalonians 5:18 In everything give thanks, for this is the
will of יהוה in Messiah Yeshua toward you.

Chapter Six: Self-Care and the Fruits of the Spirit

[1]Philippians 1:6 …being confident of this very thing, that He
who began a good work in you will complete it until the day of
Yeshua Messiah.

[2]Proverbs 16:9 A man's heart plans his course, but Adonai
directs his steps.

[3]Matthew 11:28-30 Come to Me, all you who labor and are
heavily burdened, and I will give you rest. Take My yoke upon
you and learn from Me, for I am gentle and humble in heart; and

you will find rest for your souls. For My yoke is easy, and My burden is light.

Chapter Seven: The Discipline of a Healthy Mind

¹2 Corinthians 10:3-5 For though we walk in the flesh, we don't wage war according to the flesh, for the weapons of our warfare are not of the flesh, but mighty before יהוה to the throwing down of strongholds, throwing down imaginations and every high thing that is exalted against the knowledge of יהוה and bringing every thought into captivity to the obedience of Yeshua.

²Hebrews 4:15 For we don't have a High Priest who can't be touched with the feeling of our infirmities, but One who has been in all points tempted like we are, yet without sin.

³Isaiah 41:10 Don't you be afraid, for I am with you. Don't be dismayed, for I am your Elohim. I will strengthen you, yes, I will help you. Yes, I will uphold you with the right hand of My righteousness.

⁴Romans 8:1 There is therefore now no condemnation for those who are in Messiah Yeshua, who don't walk according to the flesh, but according to the Spirit.

⁵Philippians 4:13 I can do all things through Yeshua who strengthens me.

⁶Ephesians 6:16 …above all, taking up the Shield of Faith, with which you will be able to quench all the fiery darts of the evil one.

Chapter Eight: Rest, Solitude and the Sabbath

[1]Genesis 2:2-3 On the seventh day Elohim finished His work which He had done; and He rested on the seventh day from all His work which He had done. Elohim blessed the seventh day, and made it holy, because He rested in it from all His work of creation which He had done.

[2]Exodus 20:8-11 Remember the Sabbath day, to keep it holy. You shall labor six days, and do all your work, but the seventh day is a Sabbath to יהוה your Elohim. You shall not do any work in it, you, nor your son, nor your daughter, your male servant, nor your female servant, nor your livestock, nor your stranger who is within your gates, for in six days Elohim made heaven and earth, the sea, and all that is in them, and rested on the seventh day; therefore Elohim blessed the Sabbath day, and made it holy

[3]Exodus 31:12-17 יהוה spoke to Moses, saying, "Speak also to the children of Israel, saying, 'Most certainly you shall keep My Sabbaths; for it is a sign between Me and you throughout your generations, that you may know that I am יהוה who sanctifies you. You shall keep the Sabbath therefore, for it is holy to you. Everyone who profanes it shall surely be put to death; for whoever does any work therein, that soul shall be cut off from among his people. Six days shall work be done, but the seventh day is a Sabbath of solemn rest, holy to יהוה. Whoever does any work on the Sabbath day shall surely be put to death. Therefore, the children of Israel shall keep the Sabbath, to observe the Sabbath throughout their generations, for a perpetual covenant. It is a sign between Me and the children of Israel forever; for in six days Elohim made heaven and earth, and on the seventh day He rested, and was refreshed.

⁴Ezekiel 20:12 Moreover I also gave them My Sabbaths, to be a sign between me and them, that they might know that I am יהוה who sanctifies them.

⁵1 Corinthians 6:19-20 Or don't you know that your body is a temple of the Holy Spirit who is in you, whom you have from יהוה? You are not your own, for you were bought with a price. Therefore, glorify יהוה in your body and in your spirit, which are יהוה's.

⁶Proverbs 3:6 In all your ways acknowledge Him, and He will make your paths straight.

⁷Proverbs 3:7-8 Don't be wise in your own eyes. Fear יהוה, and depart from evil. It will be health to your body, and nourishment to your bones.

⁸Mark 1:35 Early in the morning, while it was still dark, He rose up and went out, and departed into a deserted place, and prayed there.

Chapter Nine: Emotional Healing and Self-Love

¹John 5:5-9 A certain man was there who had been sick for thirty-eight years. When Yeshua saw him lying there, and knew he had been sick for a long time, He asked him, "Do you want to be made well?" The sick man answered Him, "Sir, I have no one to put me into the pool when the water is stirred up, but while I'm coming, another steps down before me." Yeshua said to him, "Arise, take up your mat, and walk." Immediately, the man was made well, and took up his mat and walked.

²Matthew 6:14-15 "For if you forgive men their trespasses, your heavenly Father will also forgive you. But if you don't forgive men their trespasses, neither will your Father forgive your trespasses.

³Matthew 18:21-22 Then Peter came and said to Him, "Rabbi, how often shall my brother sin against me, and I forgive him. Until seven times? Yeshua said to him, "I don't tell you until seven times, but, until seventy times seven.

⁴Colossians 3:12-13 Put on therefore, as יהוה's chosen ones, holy and beloved, a heart of compassion, kindness, lowliness, humility, and perseverance; bearing with one another, and forgiving each other, if any man has a complaint against any; even as Yeshua forgave you, so you also do.

⁵Isaiah 61:1-3 יהוה 's Spirit is on me, because יהוה has anointed me to preach good news to the humble. He has sent me to bind up the broken hearted, to proclaim liberty to the captives and release to those who are bound, to proclaim the Year of יהוה 's favor and the day of vengeance of our Elohim, to comfort all who mourn, to provide for those who mourn in Zion, to give them a garland for ashes, the oil of joy for mourning, the garment of praise for the spirit of heaviness, that they may be called trees of righteousness, the planting of יהוה, that He may be glorified.

⁶Romans 8:28 We know that all things work together for good for those who love יהוה, for those who are called according to His purpose.

⁷Genesis 50:20 As for you, you meant evil against me, but יהוה meant it for good, to save many people alive, as is happening today.

Chapter Ten: Forgiveness of Self and Others

¹"Resentment is like drinking poison and waiting for the other person to die." Saint Augustine

²Psalm 103:8-14

יהוה is merciful and gracious,
slow to anger, and abundant in loving kindness.
He will not always accuse;
neither will He stay angry forever.
He has not dealt with us according to our sins,
nor repaid us for our iniquities.
For as the heavens are high above the earth,
so great is His loving kindness toward those who fear Him.
As far as the east is from the west,
so far has He removed our transgressions from us.
Like a father has compassion on his children,
so יהוה has compassion on His children,
for יהוה has compassion on those who fear Him.
For He knows how we are made.
He remembers that we are dust.

³Luke 23:34 Yeshua said, "Father, forgive them, for they don't know what they are doing."

Chapter Eleven: The Outpouring of Self-Care

¹*Kehilah* means congregation or community.

²Proverbs 27:17 Iron sharpens iron; so a man sharpens his friend's countenance.

³Hebrews 10:24 Let's consider how to provoke one another to love and good works.

⁴Titus 2:1-8 But say the things which fit sound doctrine, that older men should be temperate, sensible, sober minded, sound in faith, in love and in perseverance, and that older women likewise be reverent in behavior, not slanderers nor enslaved to much

wine, teacher of that which is good, that they may train the young wives to love their husbands, to love their children, to be sober minded, chaste, workers at home, kind, being in subjection to their own husbands, that יהוה's word may not be blasphemed. Likewise, exhort the younger men to be sober minded. In all things show integrity, seriousness, incorruptibility, and soundness of speech that can't be condemned, that he who opposes you may be ashamed, having no evil thing to say about us.

[5]1 Timothy 3:4-5 not a drinker, not violent, not greedy for money, but gentle, not quarrelsome, not covetous, one who rules his own house well, having children in subjection with all reverence; (for how could someone who doesn't know how to rule his own house take care of יהוה's assembly?)

[6]*Teshuvah* appears nearly 1,000 times in Scripture. It means to "turn back" or "return". It is commonly used to describe "turning away from wrongdoing and returning to יהוה." This word is used most often to convey repentance. Strong's #H8666

[7]Luke 15:11-32 He said, "A certain man had two sons. The younger of them said to his father, 'Father, give me my share of your property.' So he divided his livelihood between them. Not many days after, the younger son gathered all of this together and traveled into a far country. There he wasted his property with riotous living. When he had spent all of it, there arose a severe famine in that country, and he began to be in need. He went and joined himself to one of the citizens of that country, and he sent him into his fields to feed pigs. He wanted to fill his belly with the pods that the pigs ate, but no one gave him any. But when he came to himself, he said, 'How many hired servants of my father's have bread enough to spare, and I'm

dying with hunger! I will get up and go to my father, and will tell him, "Father, I have sinned against heaven and in your sight. I am no more worthy to be called your son. Make me as one of your hired servants." '

"He arose and came to his father. But while he was still far off, his father saw him and was moved with compassion, and ran, fell on his neck, and kissed him. The son said to him, 'Father, I have sinned against heaven and in your sight. I am no longer worthy to be called your son.'

"But the father said to his servants, 'Bring out the best robe and put it on him. Put a ring on his hand and sandals on his feet. Bring the fattened calf, kill it, and let's eat and celebrate; for this, my son, was dead and is alive again. He was lost and is found.' Then they began to celebrate.

"Now his elder son was in the field. As he came near to the house, he heard music and dancing. He called one of the servants to him and asked what was going on. He said to him, 'Your brother has come, and your father has killed the fattened calf, because he has received him back safe and healthy.' But he was angry and would not go in. Therefore his father came out and begged him. But he answered his father, 'Behold, these many years I have served you, and I never disobeyed a commandment of yours, but you never gave me a goat, that I might celebrate with my friends. But when this your son came, who has devoured your living with prostitutes, you killed the fattened calf for him.'

"He said to him, 'Son, you are always with me, and all that is mine is yours. But it was appropriate to celebrate and be glad, for this, your brother, was dead, and is alive again. He was lost, and is found.'"

[8]*The Shema* is a declaration of faith that is recited twice daily, in the morning and evening as an affirmation of identity as

YHVH's people, and commitment to keeping His ways. The Shema comes from both Deuteronomy 11:13-21 and Numbers 15:37-41.

[9]Deuteronomy 6:4-9 Hear, Israel: יהוה is our Elohim. Elohim is one. You shall love יהוה your Elohim with all your heart, with all your soul, and with all your might. These words, which I command you today, shall be on your heart; and you shall teach them diligently to your children, and shall talk of them when you sit in your house, and when you walk by the way, and when you lie down, and when you rise up. You shall bind them for a sign on your hand, and they shall be for frontlets between your eyes. You shall write them on the door posts of your house and on your gates.

[10]Numbers 15:37-41 יהוה spoke to Moses, saying, "Speak to the children of Israel, and tell them that they should make themselves fringes on the borders of their garments throughout their generations, and that they put on the fringe of each border a cord of blue. It shall be to you for a fringe, that you may see it, and remember all יהוה's commandments, and do them; and that you don't follow your own heart and your own eyes, after which you used to play the prostitute; so that you may remember and do all My commandments, and be holy unto your Elohim. I am יהוה your Elohim, who brought you out of the land of Egypt, to be your Elohim: I am יהוה your Elohim."

Afterward

[1]Acts 17:28 For in Him we live, move and have our being.

About the Author

S.T. Arriaga, who also writes as Shann Tajiah, is an award-winning poet and author. With a deep passion for storytelling and creative expression, she has authored multiple works, including *The Shaloma*, *Scraps of Love*, and *The Author Platform Roadmap*. Through her writing, she explores themes of redemption, healing, and love, crafting narratives that challenge old ways of thinking and uplift the spirit.

As the founder of Ithirial Rising Press and Kadesh Ink Author Services, Shann is dedicated to supporting fellow authors in their publishing journeys through coaching and creative development.

Originally from Minnesota, she now resides in West Central Texas with her husband, their lively dog Frolic, and their easygoing cat Jakob. When not writing she works as an Activity Director in Long-term care, and enjoys music, cooking, tending to her garden, and finding inspiration in quiet moments in her hammock.

You can connect with Shann on YouTube and Facebook @authorshanntajiah and at www.shanntajiah.com.

Other Titles Available from Ithirial Rising Press

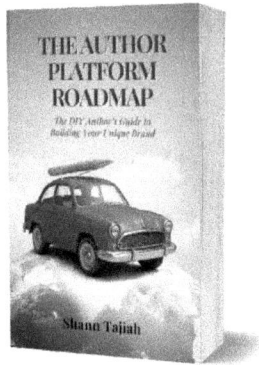

The Author Platform Roadmap:
The DIY Author's Guide to Building Your Unique Brand
Shann Tajiah

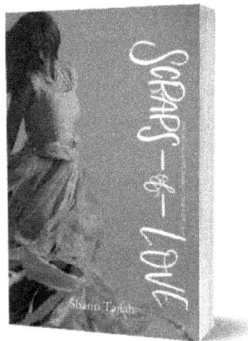

Scraps of Love: Poetry from the Darkest Night 1997-2010
Shann Tajiah

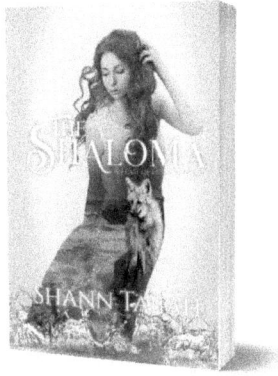

East of Eeden Book One: The Shaloma
Shann Tajiah

www.ingramcontent.com/pod-product-compliance
Lightning Source LLC
Chambersburg PA
CBHW062001040426
42447CB00010B/1853